PN
6110
.B6
S4

Scoll

T4-AEI-322

The bird-lovers'
anthology

OAKLAND COMMUNITY COLLEGE
ORCHARD RIDGE LIBRARY
27055 ORCHARD LAKE ROAD
FARMINGTON, MICHIGAN 48024

THE BIRD-LOVERS'
ANTHOLOGY

THE BIRD-LOVERS' ANTHOLOGY

COMPILED BY
CLINTON SCOLLARD
AND
JESSIE B. RITTENHOUSE

BOSTON AND NEW YORK
HOUGHTON MIFFLIN COMPANY
The Riverside Press Cambridge
1930

COPYRIGHT, 1930, BY HOUGHTON MIFFLIN COMPANY

ALL RIGHTS RESERVED

The Riverside Press
CAMBRIDGE · MASSACHUSETTS
PRINTED IN THE U.S.A.

FOREWORD

It will be of interest to the bird-lover to recall that the first recorded English lyric bearing any distinctive charm is a cuckoo song:

> *Summer is i-comen in,*
> *Loud sing cuckoo.*

From the time, seven hundred years ago it is conjectured, when the unknown lyrist penned this song until the present day, scarcely a poet has written who has not in some wise celebrated the birds. Witness Chaucer with his

> *Smale foweles maken melodye —*

Shakespeare with his

> *Hark, hark, the lark —*

Milton addressing the nightingale:

> *O nightingale that on yon bloomy spray —*

Even the starched and precise Pope, hearing song borne in through the open casement of his Twickenham villa, exclaims,

> *Why sit we mute when early linnets sing?*

These, to name no more from the earlier poets, attest to the charm exercised by the little brothers of the air. The later singers have written with equal feeling and more voluminously of the birds, but it has been necessary to make this collection selective rather than inclusive, although it is hoped that no notable bird poem will be found lacking.

CLINTON SCOLLARD
JESSIE B. RITTENHOUSE

ACKNOWLEDGMENTS

Thanks are due to the following publishers, editors, and authors for their kind permission to use the poems included in this volume:

D. Appleton and Company, for "Chickadee," from *The Home Road*, by Martha Haskell Clark, and for "The Herons on Bo Island," from *By Bog and Sea in Donegal*, by Elizabeth Shane.

The Bookfellows, for "The Humming Bird" and "The Sandpiper," from *Fagots of Cedar*, by Ivan Swift.

Albert and Charles Boni, Inc., for "The Thrush," from *Faery Bread*, by Laura Benét, and for "Turkey-Buzzards," from 7 *P.M. and Other Poems*, by Mark Van Doren.

Boni and Liveright, for "Birds," from *Roan Stallion, Tamar, and Other Poems*, by Robinson Jeffers, and for "Owl Sinister," from *The Master Mistress*, by Rose O'Neill.

Brentano's, Inc., for "To a Sparrow," by Francis Ledwidge.

Jonathan Cape and Harrison Smith, for "The Hawk" and "The Kingfisher," by William H. Davies.

The Century Company, for "To a Petrel" and "To a Solitary Seagull," from *Selected Plays and Poems*, by Cale Young Rice, and for "Serfs," from *Stygian Freight*, by the same author.

Doubleday, Doran and Company, for "The Bird of Paradise," by Laura Benét, from *Noah's Dove*, copyrighted, 1929, by Doubleday, Doran and Company, Inc.; for "Birds," by J. C. Squire, from *Poems: Second Series*, copyrighted, 1920, 1921, by Doubleday, Doran and Company, Inc.; and for "Joy of the Morning," from *The Man with the Hoe, and Other Poems*, by Edwin Markham.

Dodd, Mead and Company, Inc., for "To a Bird at Dawn," from *The Lonely Dancer*, and "The Cuckoo," from *New Poems*, by Richard Le Gallienne.

ACKNOWLEDGMENTS

E. P. Dutton and Company, for "Swallow," from *A Canopic Jar*, by Leonora Speyer.

Harper and Brothers, for "The Swan," from *Atlas and Beyond*, by Elizabeth Coatsworth; for "A Blackbird Suddenly," "Berceuse for Birds," and "Is This the Lark," from *Sunrise Trumpets*, by Joseph Auslander; and for "On First Having Heard the Skylark," from *The Buck in the Snow*, by Edna St. Vincent Millay.

Henry Holt and Company, for "The Two Nests," from *The Cairn of Stars*, by Francis Carlin; for "A Minor Bird," from *West Running Brook*, and "The Oven Bird," from *Mountain Interval*, by Robert Frost; for "The Blackbird," from *A Shropshire Lad*, by A. E. Housman; for "The Linnet," from *Collected Poems*, by Walter de la Mare; and for "The Loon," from *Many, Many Moons*, and "To a Wild Goose over Decoys," from *Slow Smoke*, by Lew Sarett.

Houghton Mifflin Company, for "The Bluebird" (extract from "Spring in New England"), from *Poems*, by Thomas Bailey Aldrich; for "The Crow," "The Downy Woodpecker," "The Swallow," and "To the Lapland Longspur," from *Bird and Bough*, by John Burroughs; for "Blackbird" and "Fairford Nightingales," from *Poems: 1908–1919*, by John Drinkwater; for "The Titmouse," from *Poems*, by Ralph Waldo Emerson; for "Doves" and "Rooks: New College Gardens," from *Happy Ending*, by Louise Imogen Guiney; for "To a Sea-Bird," from *Poems*, by Bret Harte; for "Purple Grackles," from *What's O'Clock*, by Amy Lowell; for "The Bobolink," from *The Biglow Papers*, by James Russell Lowell; for "The Nightingale Unheard," from *The Singing Man*, by Josephine Preston Peabody; for "White Peacocks," from *The Door of Dreams*, by Jessie B. Rittenhouse; for "The Goldfinch," from *A Lonely Flute*, by Odell Shepard; for "The Village Stork," from *Poems*, by Bayard Taylor; and for "The Bluebird," "The Blue Heron," "The Humming Bird," and "Spring's Torch Bearer," from *Poems*, by Maurice Thompson.

Alfred A. Knopf, Inc., for "The Tree of Starlings," from *Ship's Log*, by Grace Hazard Conkling, and for "A Thrush in the Moonlight," "The Sandpiper," and "To a Phœbe Bird," from *Grenstone Poems*, by Witter Bynner.

Little, Brown and Company, for "The Bluebird" and "The Robin," from *Poems*, by Emily Dickinson.

ACKNOWLEDGMENTS

The Macmillan Company, for "The Rain-Crow," from *Poems*, by Madison Cawein; for "Golden Falcon," from *Golden Falcon*, by Robert P. Tristram Coffin; for "The Blue Jay," from *The Garden of the West*, by Louise Driscoll; for "A Bird Sings at Night" and "The Owl," from *Time's Profile*, by Hildegarde Flanner; for "The Courtyard Pigeons," from *The Veiled Door*, by Caroline Giltinan; for "The Darkling Thrush," from *Collected Poems*, by Thomas Hardy; for "Stupidity Street," from *Poems*, by Ralph Hodgson; for "The Song Sparrow" and "The Upland Plover," from *Collected Poems*, by Percy MacKaye; for "The Water Ouzel," from *You and I*, by Harriet Monroe; for "Birds," from *Songs of the Glens of Antrim*, by Moira O'Neill; for "Bird Music," from *Children of the Sun*, by James Rorty; for "Red Birds" and "Wood Song," from *Flame and Shadow*, by Sara Teasdale; for "The Lesser Children," from *Hesperides*, by Ridgely Torrence; and for "The Wild Swans at Coole," from *Later Poems*, by William Butler Yeats.

Thomas B. Mosher, for "The Birds of Whitby," from *Sonnets of the Saints*, by Thomas S. Jones, Jr., and for "The Lark," from *A Wayside Lute*, by Lizette Woodworth Reese.

G. P. Putnam's Sons, for "On Hearing a Bird Sing at Night," from *Ships in Harbor*, by David Morton.

A. M. Robertson, for "The Black Vulture," by George Sterling.

Small, Maynard and Company, for "The Rainbird," from *April Airs*, by Bliss Carman, and for "The Mocking Bird," from *More Songs from Vagabondia*, by Richard Hovey.

Charles Scribner's Sons, for "A Late Lark" and "The Blackbird," by William Ernest Henley; for "The Mocking Bird," by Sidney Lanier; for "A Thrush Before Dawn," by Alice Meynell; for "The Veery," by Henry van Dyke; and for "The Fish-Hawk," by John Hall Wheelock.

The Unicorn Press, for "Pretty Polly," from *Lost Eden, and Other Poems*, by E. Merrill Root.

The Viking Press, for "Pigeons," from *A Boy in the Wind*, by George Dillon.

Harold Vinal, Limited, for "The Fox Sparrow," "The Mourning Dove," and "The Snow Lies Light," from *Songs of the Helderhills*, by W. W. Christman, and for "To a Scarlet Tanager," from *Cliff Dwellings, and Other Poems*, by Glenn Ward Dresbach.

ACKNOWLEDGMENTS

James T. White and Company, for "To a Grosbeak in the Garden," from *The Blue Crane, and Shore Songs*, by Ivan Swift; for "Spring Song" and "Canticle," from *City Pastorals, and Other Poems*, by William Griffith; and for "The Downy Owl," from *A Cycle of Sonnets*, by Edith Willis Linn.

The Yale University Press, for "Overtones," from *In April Once*, by William Alexander Percy, and for "Thrushes," from *Blue Smoke*, by Karle Wilson Baker.

Harper's Magazine, for "Swans," by Leonora Speyer; *The New Republic*, for "Happy is He," by Leonora Speyer; *The Sun* (New York), for "Purple Grackles," by Frances M. Frost; Books (*New York Herald-Tribune*), for "Hawk Afield," by Evelyn Scott; *The Ladies' Home Journal*, for "Morning Bird," by Louis Untermeyer; *The Saturday Review of Literature*, for "Night-Hawk," by Robert P. Tristram Coffin; *The Yale Review*, for "Humming Bird," by Robert P. Tristram Coffin; *The Century Magazine*, for "Crow," by Mark Van Doren, "Blue Jay," by Leonora Speyer, and "The Wild Duck," by Leroy McLeod.

The compilers wish to thank personally the following poets who have graciously given special permission for the use of copyrighted material: W. W. Christman, Glenn Ward Dresbach, Herbert Gorman, William Griffith, Thomas S. Jones, Jr., Hamlin Garland, Edwin Markham, Whitney Montgomery, David Morton, Frederick Peterson, Lizette Woodworth Reese, Cale Young Rice, E. Merrill Root, Leonora Speyer, Rose O'Neill, Ivan Swift, and Mark Van Doren; and also those who have kindly allowed us to include poems not yet in book form: Irving Bacheller, Ralph Cheyney, Robert P. Tristram Coffin, Philip Cummings, Frances M. Frost, Hilton R. Greer, William Griffith, Grace Noll Crowell, Edwin Osgood Grover, Brenham McKay, Rose Mills Powers, Lew Sarett, Rena Sheffield, Evelyn Scott, Elisabeth Scollard, Leonora Speyer, James B. Thomas, Louis Untermeyer, and Halle W. Warlow.

CONTENTS

THE BIRD FAMILY

Pack, Clouds, Away. *Thomas Heywood*	3
A Health to the Birds. *Seumas MacManus*	3
A Minor Bird. *Robert Frost*	5
Overtones. *William Alexander Percy*	6
Bird Music. *James Rorty*	6
Return to Birds. *Louis Untermeyer*	7
The Bird at Dawn. *Harold Monro*	11
To a Bird at Dawn. *Richard Le Gallienne*	12
Happy Is He. *Leonora Speyer*	14
Morning Bird. *Louis Untermeyer*	14
Bird Song. *Alfred Noyes*	15
Joy of the Morning. *Edwin Markham*	17
To a Bird on a Downtown Wire. *Hilton Ross Greer*	18
Poet to Bird. *Ralph Cheyney*	18
The Two Nests. *Francis Carlin*	19
A Caged Bird. *Sarah Orne Jewett*	19
On the Death of a Favourite Canary. *Matthew Arnold*	21
Three Things to Remember. *William Blake*	22
Stupidity Street. *Ralph Hodgson*	22
A Flaw. *Michael Field*	23
The Birds. *J. C. Squire*	23
Birds. *Robinson Jeffers*	26
The Birds. *Herbert Gorman*	27
The Birds of Whitby. *Thomas S. Jones, Jr.*	28

BLITHE NEW COMERS

Cuckoo Song. *Anonymous*	31
To the Cuckoo. *William Wordsworth*	31
Cuckoo. *Katherine Tynan Hinkson*	32
The Cuckoo. *Richard Le Gallienne*	33

CONTENTS

The Rainbird. *Bliss Carman*	34
Robin Song. *Elisabeth Scollard*	35
The Robin. *Emily Dickinson*	35
Birds. *Moira O'Neill*	36
The Tryst. *Whitney Montgomery*	37
The Bluebird. *Thomas Bailey Aldrich*	38
Spring Song. *William Griffith*	38
The Bluebird. *Emily Dickinson*	39
The Bluebird. *Maurice Thompson*	39
Blue Jay. *Leonora Speyer*	41
The Blue Jay. *Louise Driscoll*	41
The Fox Sparrow. *W. W. Christman*	42
To a Sparrow. *Francis Ledwidge*	43
The Song-Sparrow. *Percy MacKaye*	44
The Swallow. *John Burroughs*	45
Swifts in the Chimney. *Rose Mills Powers*	47
Itylus. *Algernon Charles Swinburne*	48

ETHEREAL MINSTRELS

Song from "Cymbeline." *William Shakespeare*	53
To the Lark. *Robert Herrick*	53
To a Skylark. *William Wordsworth*	54
The Skylark. *James Hogg*	55
To a Skylark. *William Wordsworth*	56
To a Skylark. *Percy Bysshe Shelley*	56
On First Having Heard the Skylark. *Edna St. Vincent Millay*	60
Is This the Lark. *Joseph Auslander*	61
The Lark. *Lizette Woodworth Reese*	62
A Word with a Skylark. *Sarah M. B. Piatt*	63
Lark's Song. *Seumas O'Sullivan*	63
From "The Lark Ascending." *George Meredith*	64
A Late Lark. *William Ernest Henley*	65
Blow Softly, Thrush. *Joseph Russell Taylor*	66
The Veery. *Henry van Dyke*	67
Thrushes. *Karle Wilson Baker*	68

CONTENTS

Wood Song. *Sara Teasdale*	68
Wood-Thrush. *Clinton Scollard*	68
Articulate Thrush. *Lew Sarett*	69
The Wood-Thrush. *John Vance Cheney*	70
The Thrush. *Laura Benét*	70
A Thrush in the Moonlight. *Witter Bynner*	71
The Wise Thrush. *Robert Browning*	71
Ballade of the Thrush. *Austin Dobson*	72
My Thrush. *Mortimer Collins*	73
A Thrush Before Dawn. *Alice Meynell*	73
The Darkling Thrush. *Thomas Hardy*	74
The Song of the Hermit Thrush. *James B. Thomas*	76
A Hermit Thrush in the Catskills. *William Griffith*	77
The Nightingale. *Richard Barnfield*	78
To the Nightingale. *John Milton*	79
Ode to a Nightingale. *John Keats*	80
Philomela. *Matthew Arnold*	83
O Nightingale! Thou Surely Art. *William Wordsworth*	84
Nightingales. *Robert Bridges*	85
Fairford Nightingales. *John Drinkwater*	85
A Damascus Nightingale. *Stephen Crombie*	86
The Nightingale Unheard. *Josephine Preston Peabody*	87

THE SUMMER CHOIR

The White-throat. *Anonymous*	93
The Oven-bird. *Robert Frost*	93
The Linnet. *Walter de la Mare*	93
To a Blue Tit. *V. H. Friedlaender*	94
Bob White. *Dora Read Goodale*	95
The Last Bob White. *Whitney Montgomery*	96
A Meadow Lark Sang. *Charles Commerford*	97
Berceuse for Birds. *Joseph Auslander*	97
Phoebe. *Anonymous*	98
To a Phoebe Bird. *Witter Bynner*	98
Goldfinches. *Elisabeth Scollard*	99
The Goldfinch. *Odell Shepard*	100

Canticle. *William Griffith*	100
The Bobolink. *James Russell Lowell*	101
Robert of Lincoln. *William Cullen Bryant*	101
To the Lapland Longspur. *John Burroughs*	104
The Rain-Crow. *Madison Cawein*	105
Magpies in Picardy. *T. P. Cameron Wilson*	107

WINGED JEWELS

To an Oriole. *Edgar Fawcett*	111
Spring's Torch-Bearer. *Maurice Thompson*	111
Redbirds. *Sara Teasdale*	113
To a Scarlet Tanager. *Glenn Ward Dresbach*	113
The Scarlet Tanager. *Joel Benton*	114
The Cardinal Bird. *William Davis Gallagher*	114
To a Grosbeak in the Garden. *Ivan Swift*	116
Indigo Bird. *Stephen Crombie*	117
Humming Bird. *Robert P. Tristram Coffin*	117
The Humming Bird. *Maurice Thompson*	118
The Humming Bird. *Ednah Proctor Clarke*	119
A Humming Bird. *Edgar Fawcett*	120
The Humming Bird. *Ivan Swift*	121

MOCKERS

The Mocking Bird. *Richard Hovey*	125
To the Mocking Bird. *Richard Henry Wilde*	125
The Mocking Bird. *Irving Bacheller*	126
The Mocking Bird. *Sidney Lanier*	127
The Flute of Krishna. *James B. Thomas*	128
To a Mocking Bird. *Edwin Osgood Grover*	129
Out of the Cradle Endlessly Rocking. *Walt Whitman*	130
My Catbird. *William Henry Venable*	138
Catbird. *Stephen Crombie*	139
To the Catbird. *Anonymous*	140

THE LESSER CHILDREN

The Lesser Children. *Ridgely Torrence*	145

CONTENTS

BIRDS OF SEA AND SHORE

To a Seamew. *Algernon Charles Swinburne*	153
To a Sea-Bird. *Francis Bret Harte*	154
Sanctuary. *Elinor MacArthur*	155
The Little Beach-Bird. *Richard Henry Dana*	155
The Sandpiper. *Celia Thaxter*	156
The Sandpiper. *Witter Bynner*	158
The Sandpiper. *Ivan Swift*	158
Sea-Stretch. *Rena Sheffield*	160
To a Sea-Gull. *Arthur Symons*	161
Sea-Gull. *Mary Carolyn Davies*	162
The Onset. *Jessie B. Rittenhouse*	162
To a Solitary Sea-Gull. *Cale Young Rice*	163
Sea-Birds. *Elizabeth Akers Allen*	163
Sea-Birds. *Elinor MacArthur*	164
Gulls Over Great Salt Lake. *Ross Sutphen*	165
The Stormy Petrel. *Bryan Waller Procter*	166
To a Petrel. *Cale Young Rice*	167
To the Man-of-War-Bird. *Walt Whitman*	167
Albatross. *Charles Warren Stoddard*	168

BIRDS OF LAKE AND RIVER, MARSH AND MOOR

The Heron. *Edward Hovell-Thurlow*	173
Dawn in the Everglades. *Halle W. Warlow*	173
The Blue Heron. *Maurice Thompson*	174
The Herons on Bo Island. *Elizabeth Shane*	175
The Village Stork. *Bayard Taylor*	176
The Herald Crane. *Hamlin Garland*	178
With the Mallard Drake. *Anonymous*	180
To a Wild Goose Over Decoys. *Lew Sarett*	181
Etching at Dusk. *Frederic Prokosch*	182
The Wild Duck. *Leroy McLeod*	182
Wild Geese. *Frederick Peterson*	182
To a Waterfowl. *William Cullen Bryant*	183

The Flight of the Geese. *Charles G. D. Roberts* . . 184
The Wild Geese Come Over No More. *Cale Young Rice* 185
Wild Geese. *Eleanor Chipp* 186
Wild Geese. *Grace Noll Crowell* 186
Gray Geese Flying. *Frederic Prokosch* 187
The Loon. *Lew Sarett* 187
The Loon. *Alfred Billings Street* 187
The Water Ouzel. *Harriet Monroe* 189
To an Upland Plover. *Percy MacKaye* 189
There are Still Kingfishers. *A. Y. Campbell* . . . 190
The Kingfisher. *William H. Davies* 191
The Swan. *Elizabeth Coatsworth* 192
Swans. *Leonora Speyer* 192
Lone Swan. *Rose Mills Powers* 193
The Wild Swans at Coole. *William Butler Yeats* . . 193

BIRDS OF THE NIGHT

A Bird Sings at Night. *Hildegarde Flanner* . . . 197
On Hearing a Bird Sing at Night. *David Morton* . . 197
A Southern Whip-poor-will. *Clinton Scollard* . . . 198
Whip-poor-will. *Philip Cummings* 199
The Whip-poor-will. *Anonymous* 199
Night-Hawk. *Robert P. Tristram Coffin* 200
The Owl. *Hildegarde Flanner* 201
The Downy Owl. *Edith Willis Linn* 201
The Owl. *Alfred Tennyson* 202
The Hornèd Owl. *Bryan Waller Procter* 203
Owl Sinister. *Rose O'Neill* 204

CLERICS

The Blackbird. *A. E. Housman* 207
The Blackbird. *William Ernest Henley* 208
The Blackbird. *Humbert Wolfe* 208
To an Irish Blackbird. *James MacAlpine* 209
Blackbird. *John Drinkwater* 210

THE BIRD FAMILY

*"Was it, as the Grecian sings,
  Birds were born the first of things,
  Before the sun, before the wind,
  Before the gods, before mankind?"*

PACK, CLOUDS, AWAY

Pack, clouds, away, and welcome day,
　With night we banish sorrow;
Sweet air blow soft, mount larks aloft
　To give my Love good-morrow!
Wings from the wind to please her mind,
　Notes from the lark I'll borrow;
Bird prune thy wing, nightingale sing,
　To give my Love good-morrow;
　　To give my Love good-morrow,
　　Notes from them both I'll borrow.

Wake from thy nest, Robin-red-breast,
　Sing birds in every furrow;
And from each hill, let music shrill
　Give my fair Love good-morrow!
Blackbird and thrush in every bush,
　Stare, linnet, and cock-sparrow!
You pretty elves, amongst yourselves
　Sing my fair Love good-morrow;
　　To give my Love good-morrow,
　　Sing birds in every furrow!
Thomas Heywood

A HEALTH TO THE BIRDS

Here's a health to the birds one and all!
A health to the birds great and small!
The birds that from hill and hedge call,
Through the highlands and islands of grey Donegal —

A HEALTH TO THE BIRDS

Here's a health to them,
Health to them,
Health to them all!

Here's a health to the mavis!
A health to the mavis that sits on the thorn,
And trolls a gay breastful to brighten the morn,
And lighten the load of the man in the corn!
May its breast ne'er be tuneless, its heart ne'er forlorn —
    A health to the mavis!

Here's a health to the leverock!
A health to the leverock that loves the blue sky!
No bog is too low, no hill is too high,
And the moor's not too poor, for the leverock to lie;
May its name and its fame and its song never die!
    A health to the leverock!

Here's a health to the linnet!
A health to the linnet that lilts on the tree,
The green little linnet so pretty to see,
The linnet whose tinkling tones gladden the lea —
High health and heart-wealth, little linnet, to thee!
    A health to the linnet!

Here's a health to the blackbird!
A health to the blackbird who hides in the bush,
In the glen far from men, where the dark rivers rush,
And rolls a full soul in the round notes that gush
From his silver-toned throat at dawning's first flush —
    A health to the blackbird!

Here's a health to the wren!
Ay, a health to the wren, too, the devil's dear pet,
Through thousands of years he's owed a black debt,
And it's often we've made the vile thummikin sweat —
But away with old scores! forgive and forget!
        Here's health to the wren!

Here's a health to the birds one and all!
A health to the birds great and small —
The birds that from hill and hedge call,
Through the highlands and islands of grey Donegal —
      Here's a health to them,
        Health to them,
          Health to them all!
                Seumas MacManus

A MINOR BIRD

I HAVE wished a bird would fly away,
And not sing by my house all day;

Have clapped my hands at him from the door
When it seemed as if I could bear no more.

The fault must partly have been in me.
The bird was not to blame for his key.

And of course there must be something wrong
In wanting to silence any song.
                Robert Frost

OVERTONES

I HEARD a bird at break of day
   Sing from the autumn trees
A song so mystical and calm,
   So full of certainties,
No man, I think, could listen long
   Except upon his knees.
Yet this was but a simple bird
   Alone, among dead trees.
               William Alexander Percy

BIRD MUSIC

THE singing of birds is as certain as the long
Stroke of the March rains on the waning snows
Of winter; when the white-throat's quiver of song
Is shaken on the wind that blows
A rippled path upon the thawing lake.
Halt if you will that clear annunciation, hush
If you can the peepers' chant, or push
Back in the twig the tender-strong
Pink buds of the willow.

Earth that awakes in leaf and flower needs
Voices no less; there is a potency that breeds
Blue-birds upon the misty air,
Flying and calling; in that slow
Ecstatic warble I can hear
Earth melting and the flow
Of climbing sap, and the incessant sound
Of seeds that whisper underground....

As mutely as an April dawn
Flowers the sky, the cherry boughs
Leap into blossom; the new leaves are born
Into the sunlight without sound....
This silence is the living seed
Of music planted in the ground
Or drifting, falling
Out of the air with the oriole's calling.

Now in the summer do I find
Myself according with the simple, blind,
Triumphant logic of the pines that rear
Gray shafts of certitude and power
From earth to heaven; here
Music is constant as the light, and strong
As that blue curve of mountain; hour on hour
The vireo's song is woven on the green
Hush of the forest.... Summer is a bright
Stain on the cloak of silence thrown
From star to star, from night to night;
Nothing shall fade it; forever sown
On the face of darkness, the late gods who reel
Beneath the sleet of frozen worlds, shall feel
A flutter of brave immutable wings....
Fire in the ice... silence that sings.

James Rorty

RETURN TO BIRDS

When cities prod me with demands
Of many minds and many hands,
When life becomes a cry of bargains
In unassimilated jargons
And men bewilder men with words,

Suddenly I remember birds:
Goldfinches, those untamed canaries,
Preferring thistle-seed to cherries,
Shaking their broken crystal notes
Carelessly out of china throats.
Robin, the Spring's first feathered offering,
Whose burly strut is free of suffering
Except in drouth when his refrain
Echoes irascibly for rain.
Every bird on every hill
Whose small tongues twist and turn and trill:
The catbird, Nature's parodist,
In whose bright mill all sounds are grist —
Cluck, coloratura, mew and squawk.
The redstart's prattle, like the talk
Flung by young brooks to tolerant stones,
Contentment strengthening their bones.
The meadow-lark's slow-troubling tones.
The oven-bird, scholastic creature,
Crying for "Teacher! Teacher! Teacher!"
The oriole, that childish bird,
Importunate to be seen and heard.
The cuckoo's constant minor third.
Blackbird with epaulets of red.
Warbler parading on his head.
The cardinal, that crimson arrow.
The chestnut-crowned staccato sparrow
Whose voice is slivered in high chips.
The thrasher's frenzied sweeps and dips.
Dun city sparrows, numerous
As Jews and more ubiquitous,
Common to every slum and park.
Swallows, those arcs within an arc.
The hummingbird's arrested spark,

RETURN TO BIRDS

Half-flame, half-flower, blossoming where
Emerald and ruby burn in air.
The nighthawk's ghostly drum, the shrill
Insistence of the whip-poor-will.
The chebec, that small plague among
The flies with Egypt on its tongue.
Swifts and their irrepressible young
To whom all chimney homes are free.
Phœbes whose domesticity
Has no concern with privacy.
The purple martin's undramatic
Ecstasy of the acrobatic.
The blue-jay, bully of the boughs,
Usurping any half-built house,
Comedian-brawler among leaves,
Roisterer, rascal, king of thieves.
The sentimental pewee's call,
Persuasive in its dying fall,
More languid than a pampered woman's.
The partridge ruffling out his summons.
Crow in his sheath of violet-jet,
A ravening scold in silhouette.
Kingbird with plume-shadowed crest,
Quirring defiance from his nest.
Fat bobolink, impetuous singer,
Who, living, is a lavish flinger
Of notes too prodigal for man,
And, dead, the gourmet's ortolan.
The yellowthroat's beseeching phrase,
Void of self-pity or self-praise.
That country questioner, the chat;
Wrens who have all the answers pat.
The tanager's abrupt rebellion,
Taunting the greenery with vermilion.

Field-sparrow's mastery of change,
An opera in himself, whose range
The ear of flesh can never know.
The subtle-patterned vireo.
Metallic lustre, grating cackle,
That marks the iridescent grackle.
Those flakes of sky let loose, rose-breasted
Bodies lightly blueberry-dusted,
New England's liveliest muezzins,
The rusty robin's colored cousins.
Always a challenge, the unweary
Crescendo of the confident veery,
That thrush of overtones. And lush
As a long waterfall, the thrush
Himself, brown hermit of the trail,
Our lark, our more than nightingale,
Surpassing interval and scale....

These are the happy ones; their breath
Is song, their element is faith.
Untouched by all the transient oddities
They do not traffic in commodities;
They neither kill for sport, nor care
What way the wind will blow, or where;
Their flight does not pollute the air;
Their mornings have no yesterdays
Who, in themselves, have infinite ways
Of turning petulance to praise;
Who never trick themselves with words....
Gratefully I return to birds.

Louis Untermeyer

THE BIRD AT DAWN

What I saw was just one eye
In the dawn as I was going:
A bird can carry all the sky
In that little button glowing.

Never in my life I went
So deep into the firmament.

He was standing on a tree,
All in blossom overflowing;
And he purposely looked hard at me,
At first, as if to question merrily:
"Where are you going?"
But next some far more serious thing to say:
I could not answer, could not look away.

Oh, that hard, round and so distracting eye:
Little mirror of all sky! —
And then the after-song another tree
Held, and sent radiating back on me.

If no man had invented human word,
And a bird-song had been
The only way to utter what we mean,
What would we men have heard,
What understood, what seen,
Between the trills and pauses, in between
The singing and the silence of a bird!

Harold Monro

TO A BIRD AT DAWN

O BIRD that somewhere yonder sings,
   In the dim hour 'twixt dreams and dawn,
Lone in the hush of sleeping things,
   In some sky sanctuary withdrawn;
Your perfect song is too like pain,
And will not let me sleep again.

I think you must be more than bird,
   A little creature of soft wings,
Not yours this deep and thrilling word —
   Some morning planet 'tis that sings;
Surely from no small feathered throat
Wells that august, eternal note.

As some old language of the dead,
   In one resounding syllable,
Says Rome and Greece and all is said —
   A simple word a child may spell;
So in your liquid note impearled
Sings the long epic of the world.

Unfathomed sweetness of your song,
   With ancient anguish at its core,
What womb of elemental wrong,
   With shudder unimagined, bore
Peace so divine — what hell hath trod
This voice that softly talks with God!

All silence in one silver flower
   Of speech that speaks not, save as speaks
The moon in heaven, yet hath power
   To tell the soul the thing it seeks,

TO A BIRD AT DAWN

And pack, as by some wizard's art,
The whole within the finite part.

To you, sweet bird, one well might feign —
   With such authority you sing
So clear, yet so profound, a strain
   Into the simple ear of spring —
Some secret understanding given
Of the hid purposes of heaven.

And all my life until this day,
   And all my life until I die,
All joy and sorrow of the way,
   Seem calling yonder in the sky;
And there is something the song saith
That makes me unafraid of death.

Now the slow light fills all the trees,
   The world, before so still and strange,
With day's familiar presences,
   Back to its common self must change,
And little gossip shapes of song
The porches of the morning throng.

Not yours with such as these to vie
   That of the day's small business sing,
Voice of man's heart and of God's sky —
   But O you make so deep a thing
Of joy, I dare not think of pain
Until I hear you sing again.

                     Richard Le Gallienne

HAPPY IS HE

Happy is he who lies awake
Because of grief that hems him round,
For he shall hear, as I have heard,
The first mild clamor of a bird
That dares the day with sound.

The soft, the gay, aggressive note!
Resolute ripple from a tree
Suddenly green, as well I know
Who watch the pale sky paler grow:
Dawn is about to be.

Dawn is to be and birds to be;
There is no room for anything
Save dawn and birds in all the sky.
Blesséd is he, thrice-blesséd I,
To share this happening.

Sleeping is good and dreams are good,
And a wide, white bed for their fickle sake;
But a bird at dawn in a greening tree,
And the sound of its fluty filigree,
Is worth the night awake.

Leonora Speyer

MORNING BIRD

This is the way of a bird:
A waking, hesitant third,
Searching for notes with an eye
On the open volume of sky.

Then, not quite ready to sing,
All of him turns to wing;
Launching his body where,
On a long, smooth bank of air,
He can slide and tailspin and float.
Now he remembers his throat —
A gurgle, a vowel, and note
Follows note like links in a chain
Of white summer rain.
Spray after spray is upthrown
(Little hosannas of tone
From a mind that has never known pain)
Till the morning service is done;
He and his song being one,
Whether he's heard or unheard.
This is the way of a bird.

Louis Untermeyer

BIRD SONG

TELL me, you
   That sing in the blackthorn,
Out of what Mind
   Your melody springs.
Is it the World-Soul
   Throbs like a fountain
Up through the throat
   Of an elf with wings?

Five sweet notes
   In a golden order,
Out of that deep realm
   Quivering through,

Flashed like a phrase
　　Of light through darkness.
But *Who* entangled them?
　　Tell me, *Who?*

You whose throats
　　In the rain-drenched orchard
Peal your joys
　　In a cadenced throng;
You whose wild notes,
　　Fettered by Beauty,
Move like the stars
　　In a rounded song;

Yours is the breath
　　But Whose is the measure,
Shaped in an ecstasy
　　Past all art?
Yours is the spending:
　　Whose is the treasure?
Yours is the blood-beat:
　　Whose is the heart?

Minstrels all
　　That have woven your housen
Of withies and twigs
　　With a Mind in-wrought,
Ye are the shuttles;
　　But out of what Darkness
Gather these thoughtless
　　Patterns of thought?

Bright eyes glance
　　Through your elfin doorways,

*Roofed with rushes,
  And lined with moss.
Whose are the voiceless
  Pangs of creation?
Yours is the wild bough;
  Whose is the Cross?*

*Carols of light
  From a lovelier kingdom,
Gleams of a music
  On earth unheard,
Scattered like dew
  By the careless wayside,
Pour through the lifted
  Throat of a bird.*
                              Alfred Noyes

JOY OF THE MORNING

I HEAR you, little bird,
Shouting a-swing above the broken wall.
Shout louder yet: no song can tell it all.
Sing to my soul in the deep, still wood:
'Tis wonderful beyond the wildest word:
I'd tell it, too, if I could.

Oft when the white still dawn
Lifted the skies and pushed the hills apart,
I've felt it like a glory in my heart,
(The world's mysterious stir)
But had no throat like yours, my bird,
Nor such a listener.
                              Edwin Markham

TO A BIRD ON A DOWNTOWN WIRE

AND so, with feet God meant should cling
    To woodland rafters
You poise upon that tensile thread
    And loose your lyric laughters.

Yet through that thread this moment runs
    A human story
More fit for art than you might find
    In all your repertory —

A theme to make a master's song
    Defy all weathers;
But not for such light throat as yours —
    Theocritus in feathers!

Hilton Ross Greer

POET TO BIRD

YOUR carol is a dewy, fragrant bloom that grows
As gently as a wild, one-touch-disrupted rose.

It barely sets the smallest leaf to quivering,
And yet your little throat can free the whole of spring!

The troubled songs we poets breathe are made, not grown.
If once like you, what have we gained that will atone?

Our heavy songs must walk while yours are free to fly.
We may have gained the earth but we have lost the sky.

Ralph Cheyney

THE TWO NESTS

The wonder was on me in Curraghmacall,
  When I was as tall as the height of your knee,
That the wren should be building a hole in the wall
  Instead of a nest in a tree.

And I still do be thinking it strange, when I pass
  A pasture that has to be evenly ploughed,
That the lark should be building a hole in the grass
  Instead of a nest in a cloud.

Francis Carlin

A CAGED BIRD

High at the window in her cage
  The old canary flits and sings,
Nor sees across the curtain pass
  The shadow of the swallow's wings.

A poor deceit and copy, this,
  Of larger lives that mark their span,
Unreckoning of wider worlds,
  Of gifts that Heaven keeps for man.

She gathers piteous bits and shreds,
  This solitary, mateless thing,
To patient build again the nest
  So rudely scattered spring by spring;

And sings her brief, unlistened songs,
  Her dreams of bird-life wild and free,
Yet never beats her prison bars
  At sound of song from bush or tree.

A CAGED BIRD

But in my busiest hours I pause,
   Held by a sense of urgent speech,
Bewildered by that spark-like soul,
   Able my very soul to reach.

She will be heard; she chirps me loud,
   When I forget those gravest cares,
Her small provision to supply,
   Clear water or her seedsman's wares.

She begs me now for that chief joy
   The round great world is made to grow, —
Her wisp of greenness. Hear her chide,
   Because my answering thought is slow!

What can my life seem like to her?
   A dull, unpunctual service mine;
Stupid before her eager call,
   Her flitting steps, her insight fine.

To open wide thy prison door,
   Poor friend, would give thee to thy foes;
And yet a plaintive note I hear,
   As if to tell how slowly goes

The time of thy long prisoning.
   Bird! does some promise keep thee sane?
Will there be better days for thee?
   Will thy soul too know life again?

Ah, none of us has more than this:
   If one true friend green leaves can reach
From out some fairer, wider place,
   And understand our wistful speech.

Sarah Orne Jewett

ON THE DEATH OF A FAVOURITE CANARY

(Extract)

Birds, companions more unknown,
Live beside us, but alone;
Finding not, do all they can,
Passage from their souls to man.
Kindness we bestow, and praise,
Laud their plumage, greet their lays;
Still, beneath their feathered breast,
Stirs a history unexpressed.
Wishes there, and feelings strong,
Incommunicably throng;
What they want we cannot guess,
Fail to track their deep distress —
Dull look on when death is nigh,
Note no change, and let them die.

Was it, as the Grecian sings,
Birds were born the first of things,
Before the sun, before the wind,
Before the gods, before mankind,
Airy, ante-mundane throng —
Witness their unworldly song!
Proof they give too, primal powers,
Of a prescience more than ours —
Teach us, while they come and go,
When to sail and when to sow.
Cuckoo calling from the hill,
Swallow skimming by the mill,
Swallows trooping in the sedge,
Starlings swirling from the hedge,
Mark the seasons, map our year,
As they show and disappear.

But, with all this travail sage
Brought from that anterior age,
Goes an unreversed decree
Whereby strange are they and we,
Making want of theirs, and plan,
Indiscernible by man.

Matthew Arnold

THREE THINGS TO REMEMBER

A ROBIN REDBREAST in a cage
Puts all Heaven in a rage.

A skylark wounded on the wing
Doth make a cherub cease to sing.

He who shall hurt the little wren
Shall never be beloved by men.

William Blake

STUPIDITY STREET

I SAW with open eyes
   Singing birds sweet
Sold in the shops
   For the people to eat,
Sold in the shops of
   Stupidity Street.

I saw in vision
   The worm in the wheat,

And in the shops nothing
   For people to eat;
Nothing for sale in
   Stupidity Street.

Ralph Hodgson

A FLAW

To give me its bright plumes they shot a jay:
On the fresh jewels, blood! Oh, sharp remorse!
The glittering symbols of the little corse
I buried where the wood was noisome, blind,
Praying that I might nevermore betray
The universe, so whole within my mind.

Michael Field

THE BIRDS

WITHIN mankind's duration, so they say,
Khephren and Ninus lived but yesterday.
Asia had no name till man was old
And long had learned the use of iron and gold;
And æons had passed, when the first corn was planted,
Since first the use of syllables was granted.

Men were on earth while climates slowly swung,
Fanning wide zones to heat and cold, and long
Subsidence turned great continents to sea,
And seas dried up, dried up interminably,
Age after age; enormous seas were dried
Amid wastes of land. And the last monsters died.

Earth wore another face. O since that prime
Man with how many works has sprinkled time!

THE BIRDS

Hammering, hewing, digging tunnels, roads;
Building ships, temples, multiform abodes.
How, for his body's appetites, his toils
Have conquered all earth's products, all her soils;
And in what thousand thousand shapes of art
He has tried to find a language for his heart!

Never at rest, never content or tired:
Insatiate wanderer, marvellously fired,
Most grandly piling and piling into air
Stones that will topple or arch he knows not where.
And yet did I, this spring, think it more strange,
More grand, more full of awe, than all that change,
And lovely and sweet and touching unto tears,
That through man's chronicled and unchronicled years,
And even into that unguessed beyond
The water-hen has nested by a pond,
Weaving dry flags into a beaten floor,
The one sure product of her only lore.
Low on a ledge above the shadowed water
Then, when she heard no men, as nature taught her,
Plashing around with busy scarlet bill
She built that nest, her nest, and builds it still.

O let your strong imagination turn
The great wheel backward, until Troy unburn,
And then unbuild, and seven Troys below
Rise out of death, and dwindle, and outflow,
Till all have passed, and none has yet been there:
Back, ever back. Our birds still crossed the air;
Beyond our myriad changing generations
Still built, unchanged, their known inhabitations.

THE BIRDS

A million years before Atlantis was
Our lark sprang from some hollow in the grass,
Some old soft hoof-print in a tussock's shade;
And the wood-pigeon's snow-white eggs were laid,
High amid green pines' sunset-colored shafts,
And rooks their villages of twiggy rafts
Set on the tops of elms, where elms grew then,
And still the thumbling tit and perky wren
Popped through the tiny doors of cozy balls
And the blackbird lined with moss his high-built
    walls;
A round mud cottage held the thrush's young,
And straws from the untidy sparrow's hung.
And, skimming fork-tailed in the evening air,
When man first was were there not martins there?
Did not those birds some human shelter crave,
And stow beneath the cornice of his cave
Their dry tight cups of clay? And from each door
Peeped on a morning wiseheads three or four.

Yes, daw and owl, curlew and crested hern,
Kingfisher, mallard, water-rail and tern,
Chaffinch and greenfinch, wagtail, stonechat, ruff,
Whitethroat and robin, fly-catcher and chough,
Missel-thrush, magpie, sparrow-hawk and jay,
Built, those far ages gone, in this year's way.
And the first man who walked the cliffs of Rame,
As I this year, looked down and saw the same
Blotches of rusty red on ledge and cleft
With gray-green spots on them, while right and left
A dizzying tangle of gulls were floating and flying,
Wheeling and crossing and darting, crying and crying,
Circling and crying, over and over and over,
Crying with swoop and hover and fall and recover.

And below on a rock against the gray sea fretted,
Pipe-necked and stationary and silhouetted,
Cormorants stood in a wise, black, equal row
Above the nests and long blue eggs we know.
O delicate chain over all the ages stretched,
O dumb tradition from what far darkness fetched:
Each little architect with its one design
Perpetual, fixed and right in stuff and line,
Each little ministrant who knows one thing,
One learned rite to celebrate the spring.
Whatever alters else on sea or shore,
These are unchanging: man must still explore.

J. C. Squire

BIRDS

THE fierce musical cries of a couple of sparrow-hawks
 hunting on the headland,
Hovering and darting, their heads northwestward,
Prick like silver arrows shot through a curtain the
 noise of the ocean
Trampling its granite; their red backs gleam
Under my window around the stone corners; nothing
 gracefuller, nothing
Nimbler in the wind. Westward the wave-gleaners,
The old gray sea-going gulls are gathered together, the
 northwest wind wakening
Their wings to the wild spirals of the wind-dance.
Fresh as the air, salt as the foam, play birds in the
 bright wind, fly falcons
Forgetting the oak and the pine-woods, come gulls
From the Carmel sands and the sands at the river-
 mouth, from Lobos and out of the limitless

THE BIRDS

Power of the mass of the sea; for a poem
Needs multitude, multitudes of thoughts, all fierce, all
    flesh-eaters, musically clamorous
Bright hawks that hover and dart headlong, and un-
    gainly
Gray hungers fledged with desire of transgression, salt-
    slimed beaks, from the sharp
Rock-shores of the world and the secret waters.
Robinson Jeffers

THE BIRDS

I THOUGHT to shoulder Time but those sad birds
Would speak forever with such fiery words,
Such spinning gusts of warning tenderness
That I was helpless in my nakedness;
And sat down in the desert where the sand
Obliterated years on every hand,
So loath was I to listen. "See," I said,
"It would be better far if I were dead,
For dead men cannot hear such lovely calls
From bitter birds by Babylonian walls."

And now while chuckling Time still nudges me
Through vague savannahs of immensity,
Speaking in heavy darkness of sharp sighs
Of my befooled and barren enterprise,
And all I was flees in a shadow-show
Of antic shapes in sad imbroglio,
I cry to hear those birds who sing no more
By crumbling wall and splintered palace door,
And search in vain to see those feathered crests
Aflare like jewels in their last year's nests.
Herbert Gorman

THE BIRDS OF WHITBY

SEA-MOSSES hide the massive architrave,
   Beneath the ruined porch a sheep-bell rings,
   And where Hild's gleeman sang to silver strings
Now sound the wailing harps of wind and wave;
But though dreams pass, the restless gulls that brave
   The bitter gales still seek the peace which clings
   To hallowed walls, and furl their foam-white wings
Along the reaches of the silent nave.

And throstles at the greening of the year
   In their wild singing weave the chants of old
     That saints have limned with many a golden bar, —
The very song the angels paused to hear
   When Cædmon knelt within the cattle-fold
     Between the moonrise and the morning star.

Thomas S. Jones, Jr.

BLITHE NEW COMERS

"O blithe new-comer! I have heard,
I hear thee and rejoice.
O cuckoo! shall I call thee bird,
Or but a wandering voice?"

CUCKOO SONG

SUMMER is i-comen in,
   Loud sing cuckoo;
Groweth seed and bloweth mead,
And springeth the wood anew.
   Sing cuckoo!
Ewe bleateth after lamb,
Loweth after calfe cow,
Bullock sterteth,
Bucke verteth,
Merrie sing cuckoo!
   Cuckoo, cuckoo;
Well thou singest, cuckoo!
Nor cease thou never now.

Anonymous

TO THE CUCKOO

O BLITHE new-comer! I have heard,
   I hear thee and rejoice.
O cuckoo! shall I call thee bird,
   Or but a wandering voice?

While I am lying on the grass
   Thy twofold shout I hear;
From hill to hill it seems to pass,
   At once far off, and near.

Though babbling only to the vale
   Of sunshine and of flowers,
Thou bringest unto me a tale
   Of visionary hours.

CUCKOO

Thrice welcome, darling of the spring!
    Even yet thou art to me
No bird, but an invisible thing,
    A voice, a mystery;

The same whom in my school-boy days
    I listened to; that cry
Which made me look a thousand ways,
    In bush, and tree, and sky.

To seek thee did I often rove
    Through woods and on the green;
And thou wert still a hope, a love;
    Still longed for, never seen.

And I can listen to thee yet;
    Can lie upon the plain
And listen, till I do beget
    That golden time again.

O blessed bird! the earth we pace
    Again appears to be
An unsubstantial, faery place;
    That is fit home for thee!

William Wordsworth

CUCKOO

His voice runs before me; I follow, it flies;
It is now in the meadow and now 'mid the skies;
So blithesome, so lightsome, now distant, now here,
And when he calls "Cuckoo," the summer is near.

THE CUCKOO

He calls back the roses, red roses that went
At the first blast of winter, so sad and forespent,
With the dew in their bosoms, young roses and dear,
And when he calls "Cuckoo," the summer is near.

I would twine him a gold cage, but what would he do,
For his world of the emerald, his bath in the blue,
And his wee feathered comrades to make him good cheer?
And when he calls "Cuckoo," the summer is near.

Now, blackbird, give over your harping of gold!
Brown thrush and green linnet, your music withhold!
The flutes of the forest are silver and clear,
But when he calls "Cuckoo," the summer is here.
Katherine Tynan Hinkson

THE CUCKOO

O cuckoo troubling yonder hill
    With call — and call — and call,
I pray you sing a little low,
    If you must sing at all.

You ghost-like bird that breaks the peace
    Of April with your cry,
Not spring you mean, for when you come
    The spring is near to die.

To me you seem a midnight bird,
    A voice of death and doom
That in the palace of the spring
    Cries from some haunted room.

The vultures tearing at my heart
  Bring no such keen a pang,
Bird with the blossom in your voice
  As though the hawthorn sang.

Richard Le Gallienne

THE RAINBIRD

I HEAR a rainbird singing
Far off. How fine and clear
His plaintive voice comes ringing
With rapture to the ear!

Over the misty wood-lots,
Across the first spring heat,
Comes the enchanted cadence,
So clear, so solemn-sweet.

How often I have hearkened
To that high pealing strain
Across the cedar barrens,
Under the soft gray rain!

How often I have wondered,
And longed in vain to know
The source of that enchantment,
That touch of human woe!

O Brother, who first taught thee
To haunt the teeming spring
With that sad mortal wisdom
Which only age can bring?

Bliss Carman

ROBIN SONG

It pulses through the twilight,
　　It echoes down the dawn,
And makes the heart remember
　　Days that are gone.

Years do not change this bird note,
　　It rings as glad to-day
As though time knew no weather
　　Unlike the May.

With links no hand can sever,
　　Intangible, yet strong,
Present and past join through the gold
　　Of robin-song.
　　　　　　　　　　Elisabeth Scollard

THE ROBIN [1]

The robin is the one
That interrupts the morn
With hurried, few, express reports
When March is scarcely on.

The robin is the one
That overflows the noon
With her cherubic quantity,
And April but begun.

The robin is the one
That speechless from her nest
Submits that home and certainty
And sanctity are best.
　　　　　　　　　　Emily Dickinson

[1] Copyright, Little, Brown and Company.

BIRDS

Sure maybe ye've heard the storm-thrush
    Whistlin' bould in March,
Before there's a primrose peepin' out,
    Or a wee red cone on the larch;
Whistlin' the sun to come out o' the cloud,
    An' the wind to come over the sea,
But for all he can whistle so clear an' loud,
    He's never the bird for me.

Sure maybe ye've seen the song-thrush
    After an April rain
Slip from in-undher the drippin' leaves,
    Wishful to sing again;
An' low wi' love when he's near the nest,
    An' loud from the top o' the tree,
But for all he can flutter the heart in your breast,
    He's never the bird for me.

Sure maybe ye've heard the cushadoo
    Callin' his mate in May,
When one sweet thought is the whole of his life,
    An' he tells it the one sweet way.
But my heart is sore at the cushadoo
    Filled wid his own soft glee,
Over an' over his "me an' you!"
    He's never the bird for me.

Sure maybe ye've heard the red-breast
    Singin' his lone on a thorn,
Mindin' himself o' the dear days lost,
    Brave wid his heart forlorn.

The time is in dark November,
  An' no spring hopes has he:
"Remember," he sings, "remember!"
  Ay, *thon's* the wee bird for me.

Moira O'Neill

THE TRYST

When the spring is fresh from the hand of God,
And my first plow furrow streaks the sod,
They follow me up and down the row,
Blackbird, Field Lark, Dove and Crow.

And with the rest is a little Kildee,
With one leg off close to his knee,
And he whistles and chirps as he hobbles along,
The happiest bird in all the throng.

For three years past this little Kildee
In the spring of the year has met with me,
And it seems as if he could tell, somehow,
The very day when I'll start my plow.

I may hunt in every conceivable spot
Just the day before, but I find him not;
But ere I have driven my plow a rod,
He is hopping around from clod to clod.

I wish he could talk, I'd question him
To tell me the way he lost his limb;
I'd ask him to tell me where he passed
The long, bleak days since I saw him last.

I hate to think that a day must be
When either I, or the little Kildee,

Must break the tryst we have kept so true
Year after year, when the spring was new.

But let that pass, we are happy now
Trailing along behind the plow,
Doing our best to bridge the span
That lies between the bird and the man.
Whitney Montgomery

THE BLUEBIRD

(From *Spring in New England*)

HARK, 'tis the bluebird's venturous strain
  High on the old fringed elm at the gate —
    Sweet-voiced, valiant on the swaying bough,
Alert, elate,
  Dodging the fitful spits of snow,
  New England's poet-laureate
Telling us Spring has come again!
Thomas Bailey Aldrich

SPRING SONG

SOFTLY at dawn a whisper stole
  Down from the Green House on the Hill,
Enchanting many a ghostly bole
  And wood-song with the ancient thrill.

Gossiping on the country-side,
  Spring and the wandering breezes say,
God has thrown Heaven open wide
  And let the bluebirds out to-day.
William Griffith

THE BLUEBIRD [1]

Before you thought of spring,
Except as a surmise,
You see, God bless his suddenness,
A fellow in the skies
Of independent hues,
A little weather-worn,
Inspiriting habiliments
Of indigo and brown.

With specimens of song,
As if for you to choose,
Discretion in the interval,
With gay delay he goes
To some superior tree
Without a single leaf,
And shouts for joy to nobody
But his seraphic self!

Emily Dickinson

THE BLUEBIRD

When ice is thawed and snow is gone,
    And racy sweetness floods the trees;
When snow-birds from the hedge have flown,
    And on the hive-porch swarm the bees, —
Drifting down the first warm wind
    That thrills the earliest days of spring,
The bluebird seeks our maple groves,
    And charms them into tasselling.

He sits among the delicate sprays,
    With mists of splendor round him drawn,

---

[1] Copyright, Little, Brown and Company.

THE BLUEBIRD

And through the spring's prophetic veil
   Sees summer's rich fulfilment dawn:
He sings, and his is nature's voice, —
   A gush of melody sincere
From that great fount of harmony
   Which thaws and runs when spring is here.

Short is his song, but strangely sweet
   To ears aweary of the low,
Dull tramp of Winter's sullen feet,
   Sandalled in ice and muffed in snow:
Short is his song, but through it runs
   A hint of dithyrambs yet to be, —
A sweet suggestiveness that has
   The influence of prophecy.

From childhood I have nursed a faith
   In bluebirds' songs and winds of spring:
They tell me, after frost and death
   There comes a time of blossoming;
And after snow and cutting sleet,
   The cold, stern mood of Nature yields
To tender warmth, when bare pink feet
   Of children press her greening fields.

Sing strong and clear, O bluebird dear!
   While all the land with splendor fills,
While maples gladden in the vales
   And plum-trees blossom on the hills:
Float down the wind on shining wings,
   And do thy will by grove and stream,
While through my life spring's freshness runs
   Like music through a poet's dream.

Maurice Thompson.

BLUE JAY

I HEAR a savage tale of you,
Raucous of voice, magnificently blue.
Cannibal bird! Whose dark, defiant note
Is answered from another throat
As bright, though out of sight.

Along the icy bough you swing,
Apostrophizing a belated spring;
And I seem not to mind
Those horrid deeds to smaller of your kind:
For as you fly,
You scatter color through a frozen sky.

Black-hearted is your breast —
But ah, the blue of that uplifted crest!
Leonora Speyer

THE BLUE JAY

VILLON among the birds is he,
A bold, bright rover, bad and free;
Yet not without such loveliness
As makes the curse upon him less.
If larkspur blossoms were a-wing,
If iris went adventuring,
Or, on some morning, we should see
Heaven bright blue chicory
Come drifting by, we would forgive
Some little sins, and let them live!

Verlaine among the birds is he,
A creature of iniquity;

And yet, what joy for one who sees
An orchid drifting through the trees!
The bluebell said a naughty word
In mischief, and there was a bird.
The blue sky laughed aloud, and we
Saw wings of lapis lazuli.
So fair a sinner surely wins
A little mercy for his sins.

Louise Driscoll

THE FOX SPARROW

THE geese drive northward
   In a long gray harrow;
Spring has come back,
   And brings the sweet fox sparrow.
(His song has pierced my heart
   Like a sharp arrow.)

Oh, willow twigs,
   With silver catkins clinging!
Oh, ruddy bird!
   Oh, liquid, loud and ringing!
(Vague is the grief, —
   It is pure joy he's singing.)

Sweetest of sparrows
   That our April pledges!
I hear his song by brooksides
   And in hedges,
(When the wild geese drive north
   In flying wedges.)

Far, far his home
   Among the shrubs and mosses
By a bleak shore
   Where the cold ocean tosses.
(He has his joy —
   I have regrets and crosses.)

I have stood long
   To hear his song of mating;
All of my year
   From this full hour I'm dating —
(Some time — some spring —
   He may not find me waiting.)

They say the world is wide;
   My vale is narrow;
Would I could follow
   With the wild geese harrow, —
(Or you could stay
   And sing again, oh, sparrow,
The song that pierced my heart
   Like a sharp arrow!)

W. W. Christman

TO A SPARROW

Because you have no fear to mingle
Wings with those of greater part,
So like me, your song I single,
Your sweet impudence of heart.

And when prouder feathers go where
Summer holds her leafy show,

You still come to us from nowhere
Like gray leaves across the snow.

In back ways where odd and end go,
To your meals you drop down sure,
Knowing every broken window
Of the hospitable poor.

There is no bird half so harmless,
None so sweetly rude as you,
None so common and so charmless,
None of virtues nude as you.

But for all your faults I love you,
For you linger with us still,
Though the wintry winds reprove you,
And the snow is on the hill.

Francis Ledwidge

THE SONG-SPARROW

When June was cool and clover long
    And birds were glad in soul and body,
I sat me down to make a song,
    And sweltered in my study:
I swinked and sweat with weary art —
To tell how merry was my heart.

With weary art and wordy choice
    I toiled, when sudden — low and breezy —
I heard a little friendly voice
    Call: *Simple, simple, so easy!*

I heard, yet sat apart in dole —
To sing how social was my soul.

In vain! — That artless voice went round
  In tiny echoes, faint and teasy.
I rose: "What toil, then, have you found
  Simple, simple, so easy?"
Dauntless, the bird, with dewy beak,
Carolled again his cool critique.

Nay, song it is a simple thing
  For hearts that seek no reason.
Relentless bird, why should you sing
  Who *are* the happy season? —
Still *why!* The root of joy I seek
While laughter ripples from your beak.

No wonder, then, the bard's pen creaks,
  The critic's drone grows wheezy,
When joy the June bird never seeks
  Is *simple, simple, so easy!*
While we, who find our Art so long,
Still make a subterfuge of song!

Percy MacKaye

THE SWALLOW

At play in April skies that spread
Their azure depths above my head,
As onward to the woods I sped,
  I heard the swallow twitter;
Oh, skater in the fields of air,
On steely wings that sweep and dare,

To gain these scenes thy only care,
  Nor fear the winds are bitter.

This call from thee is tidings dear,
The news that crowns the vernal year,
'Tis true, 'tis true, the swallow's here,
  The south wind brings her greeting;
Thy voice is neither call nor song,
And yet it starts a varied throng
Of fancies sweet and memories long, —
  It sounds like lovers meeting.

I know thou dost not kiss on wing,
I know thou dost not pipe or sing,
Or bill or coo, in early spring,
  And yet these sounds ecstatic;
Thy ruddy breast from over seas,
Like embers quickened by the breeze,
Now feels the warmth of love's decrees
  That make thy joy emphatic.

Ah, well I know thy deep-dyed vest,
Thy burnished wing, thy feathered nest,
Thy lyric flight at love's behest,
  And all thy ways so airy.
Thou art a nursling of the air,
No earthly food makes up thy fare,
But soaring things both frail and rare, —
  Fit diet of a fairy.

I see thee sit upon the ground
And stoop and stare and hobble round,
As if thy silly legs were bound,
  Or it were freezing weather;

Thou hast but little need of feet, —
To gather mortar for thy seat,
To perch on wires above the street,
   Or pick up straw or feather.

Kind nature gave thee power of flight,
And sheen of plume and iris bright,
And everything that was thy right,
   And thou art well contented;
In August days thy young are grown,
Then southward turn to warmer zone,
And follow where thy mates have flown,
   But leave our love cemented.

John Burroughs

SWIFTS IN THE CHIMNEY

I LIFT the latch
To the empty house,
Something stirring,
Is it a mouse?
Then I catch
A sound of chirring,

Little wings
In frantic whirring,
And the hungry
Clamorous twitterings
Of a young swift
Fallen from its nest,
High in the chimney, facing west.

As I lift,
With sorrow stirred

For its poignant fright,
The fledgling bird,
Back to its nest,
Secure, at rest;
As I light
At the hearth no fire,
Consuming, dire,
Till the swift takes flight;
The Voice enfolding earth and sea
Speaks in pitying majesty:
"Shall man than his God more merciful be?"

Rose Mills Powers

ITYLUS

Swallow, my sister, O sister swallow,
  How can thine heart be full of the spring?
    A thousand summers are over and dead.
What hast thou found in the spring to follow?
  What hast thou found in thine heart to sing?
    What wilt thou do when the summer is shed?

O swallow, sister, O fair swift swallow,
  Why wilt thou fly after spring to the south,
    The soft south whither thy heart is set?
Shall not the grief of the old time follow?
  Shall not the song thereof cleave to thy mouth?
    Hast thou forgotten ere I forget?

Sister, my sister, O fleet sweet swallow,
  Thy way is long to the sun and the south;
    But I, fulfilled of my heart's desire,

ITYLUS

Shedding my song upon height, upon hollow,
   From tawny body and sweet small mouth
     Feed the heart of the night with fire.

I the nightingale all spring through,
   O swallow, sister, O changing swallow,
     All spring through till the spring be done,
Clothed with the light of the night on the dew,
   Sing, while the hours and the wild birds follow,
     Take flight and follow and find the sun.

Sister, my sister, O soft light swallow,
   Though all things feast in the spring's guest-chamber,
     How hast thou heart to be glad thereof yet?
For where thou fliest I shall not follow,
   Till life forget and death remember,
     Till thou remember and I forget.

Swallow, my sister, O singing swallow,
   I know not how thou hast heart to sing.
     Hast thou the heart? is it all passed over?
Thy lord the summer is good to follow,
   And fair the feet of thy lover the spring:
     But what wilt thou say to the spring thy lover?

O swallow, sister, O fleeting swallow,
   My heart in me is a molten ember
     And over my head the waves have met.
But thou wouldst tarry or I would follow
   Could I forget or thou remember,
     Couldst thou remember and I forget.

ITYLUS

O sweet stray sister, O shifting swallow,
  The heart's division divideth us.
    Thy heart is light as a leaf of a tree;
But mine goes forth among sea-gulfs hollow
  To the place of the slaying of Itylus,
    The feast of Daulis, the Thracian sea.

O swallow, sister, O rapid swallow,
  I pray thee sing not a little space.
    Are not the roofs and the lintels wet?
The woven web that was plain to follow,
  The small slain body, the flower-like face,
    Can I remember if thou forget?

O sister, sister, thy first-begotten!
  The hands that cling and the feet that follow,
    The voice of the child's blood crying yet,
Who hath remembered me? who hath forgotten?
  Thou hast forgotten, O summer swallow,
    But the world shall end when I forget.

Algernon Charles Swinburne

ETHEREAL MINSTRELS

"Ethereal minstrel! pilgrim of the sky!"

Song from **CYMBELINE**

Hark! hark! the lark at heaven's gate sings,
   And Phœbus 'gins arise,
His steeds to water at those springs
   On chaliced flowers that lies;
And winking Mary-buds begin
   To ope their golden eyes:
With everything that pretty is,
   My lady sweet, arise:
     Arise, arise!

William Shakespeare

TO THE LARK

Good speed, for I this day
Betimes my Mattens say:
   Because I doe
   Begin to wooe:
   Sweet singing Lark,
   Be thou the Clark,
   And know thy when
   To say, *Amen*.
   And if I prove
   Blest in my love;
   Then thou shalt be
   High-Priest to me,
   At my returne,
   To Incense burne;
And so to solemnize
Love's, and my Sacrifice.

Robert Herrick

TO A SKYLARK

Up with me! up with me into the clouds!
  For thy song, Lark, is strong;
Up with me! up with me into the clouds!
  Singing, singing,
With clouds and sky about thee ringing,
Lift me, guide me till I find
That spot which seems so to thy mind!

I have walked through wildernesses dreary,
And to-day my heart is weary;
Had I now the wings of a Faery,
Up to thee I would fly.
There's madness about thee, and joy divine
In that song of thine;
Lift me, guide me high and high
To thy banqueting-place in the sky.

Joyous as morning,
Thou art laughing and scorning;
Thou hast a nest for thy love and thy rest,
And, though little troubled with sloth,
Drunken Lark! thou would'st be loth
To be such a traveller as I.
Happy, happy liver,
With a soul as strong as a mountain river
Pouring out praise to the Almighty Giver,
Joy and jollity be with us both!

Alas! my journey, rugged and uneven,
Through prickly moors or dusty ways must wind,
But hearing thee, or others of thy kind,
As full of gladness and as free of heaven,

I, with my fate contented, will plod on,
And hope for higher raptures when life's day is done.
William Wordsworth

THE SKYLARK

    BIRD of the wilderness,
    Blithesome and cumberless,
Sweet be thy matin o'er moorland and lea!
    Emblem of happiness,
    Blest is thy dwelling-place —
O to abide in the desert with thee!
    Wild is thy lay and loud
    Far in the downy cloud,
Love gives it energy, love gave it birth.
    Where, on thy dewy wing,
    Where art thou journeying?
Thy lay is in heaven, thy love is on earth.

    O'er fell and fountain sheen,
    O'er moon and mountain green,
O'er the red streamer that heralds the day,
    Over the cloudlet dim,
    Over the rainbow's rim,
Musical cherub, soar, singing, away!
    Then, when the gloaming comes,
    Low in the heather blooms,
Sweet will thy welcome and bed of love be!
    Emblem of happiness,
    Blest is thy dwelling-place —
O to abide in the desert with thee!
James Hogg

TO A SKYLARK

Ethereal minstrel! pilgrim of the sky!
Dost thou despise the earth where cares abound?
Or, while the wings aspire, are heart and eye
Both with thy nest upon the dewy ground?
Thy nest which thou canst drop into at will,
Those quivering wings composed, that music still!

To the last point of vision, and beyond,
Mount, daring warbler! that love-prompted strain,
'Twixt thee and thine a never-failing bond,
Thrills not the less the bosom of the plain:
Yet might'st thou seem, proud privilege! to sing
All independent of the leafy spring.

Leave to the nightingale her shady wood;
A privacy of glorious light is thine;
Whence thou dost pour upon the world a flood
Of harmony, with instinct more divine;
Type of the wise who soar, but never roam;
True to the kindred points of heaven and home!

William Wordsworth

TO A SKYLARK

Hail to thee, blithe spirit!
   Bird thou never wert,
That from heaven, or near it,
   Pourest thy full heart
In profuse strains of unpremeditated art.

  Higher still and higher
    From the earth thou springest

TO A SKYLARK

Like a cloud of fire;
   The blue deep thou wingest,
And singing still dost soar, and soaring ever singest.

In the golden lightning
   Of the sunken sun,
O'er which clouds are bright'ning,
   Thou dost float and run;
Like an unbodied joy whose race is just begun.

The pale purple even
   Melts around thy flight;
Like a star of heaven
   In the broad daylight
Thou art unseen, but yet I hear thy shrill delight.

Keen as are the arrows
   Of that silver sphere,
Whose intense lamp narrows
   In the white dawn clear,
Until we hardly see, we feel that it is there.

All the earth and air
   With thy voice is loud,
As, when night is bare,
   From one lonely cloud
The moon rains out her beams, and heaven is overflowed.

What thou art we know not;
   What is most like thee?
From rainbow clouds there flow not
   Drops so bright to see
As from thy presence showers a rain of melody.

TO A SKYLARK

Like a poet hidden
   In the light of thought,
Singing hymns unbidden
   Till the world is wrought
To sympathy with hopes and fears it heeded not:

Like a high-born maiden
   In a palace tower,
Soothing her love-laden
   Soul in secret hour
With music sweet as love, which overflows her bower:

Like a glow-worm golden
   In a dell of dew,
Scattering unbeholden
   Its aerial hue
Among the flowers and grass, which screen it from the view:

Like a rose embowered
   In its own green leaves,
By warm winds deflowered,
   Till the scent it gives
Makes faint with too much sweet these heavy-wingèd thieves:

Sound of vernal showers
   On the twinkling grass,
Rain-awakened flowers,
   All that ever was
Joyous, and clear, and fresh, thy music doth surpass.

Teach us, sprite or bird,
   What sweet thoughts are thine:

TO A SKYLARK

I have never heard
    Praise of love or wine
That panted forth a flood of rapture so divine.

Chorus hymeneal,
    Or triumphal chaunt,
Matched with thine would be all
    But an empty vaunt —
A thing wherein we feel there is some hidden want.

What objects are the fountains
    Of thy happy strain?
What fields, or waves, or mountains?
    What shapes of sky or plain?
What love of thine own kind? what ignorance of pain?

With thy clear keen joyance
    Languor cannot be:
Shadow of annoyance
    Never came near thee:
Thou lovest; but ne'er knew love's sad satiety.

Waking or asleep,
    Thou of death must deem
Things more true and deep
    Than we mortals dream,
Or how could thy notes flow in such a crystal stream?

We look before and after,
    And pine for what is not:
Our sincerest laughter
    With some pain is fraught;
Our sweetest songs are those that tell of saddest thought.

Yet if we could scorn
  Hate, and pride, and fear;
If we were things born
  Not to shed a tear,
I know not how thy joys we ever should come near.

Better than all measures
  Of delightful sound,
Better than all treasures
  That in books are found,
Thy skill to poet were, thou scorner of the ground!

Teach me half the gladness
  That thy brain must know,
Such harmonious madness
  From my lips would flow,
The world should listen then, as I am listening now.
                    Percy Bysshe Shelley

ON FIRST HAVING HEARD THE SKYLARK

Not knowing he rose from earth, not having seen him
    rise,
Not knowing the fallow furrow was his home,
And that high wing, untouchable, untainted,
A wing of earth, with the warm loam
Closely acquainted,
I shuddered at his cry and caught my heart.
Relentless out of heaven his sweet crying like a crystal
    dart
Was launched against me. Scanning the empty sky
I stood with thrown-back head until the world reeled.
Still, still he sped his unappeasable shafts against my
    breast without a shield.

He cried forever from his unseen throat
Between me and the sun.
He would not end his singing, he would not have done.
"Serene and pitiless note, whence, whence are you?"
I cried. "Alas, these arrows how fast they fall!
Ay, me, beset by angels in unequal fight,
Alone high on the shaven down surprised, and not a tree in sight!"
Even as I spoke he was revealed
Above me in the bright air,
A dark articulate atom in the mute enormous blue,
A mortal bird, flying and singing in the morning there.
Even as I spoke I spied him, and I knew,
And called him by his name;
"Blithe spirit!" I cried. Transfixed by more than mortal spears
I fell; I lay among the foreign daisies pink and small,
And wept, staining their innocent faces with fast-flowing tears.

Edna St. Vincent Millay

IS THIS THE LARK

Is this the lark
   Lord Shakespere heard
Out of the dark
   Of dawn? Is this the bird
   That stirred
Lord Shakespere's heart?

Is this the bird whose wing,
Whose rapturous antheming,
Rose up, soared radiant, became
Sharp flame

To Shelley listening
And made him sing,
Throbbing alone, aloof, feveredly apart,
His profuse strains of unpremeditated art?

To think that I should hear him now
    Telling that single fiery rift of heaven a wild lark
        comes!...
The fresh cool scent of earth yearns at the plow;
    In short keen rapid flurries the woodpecker drums...
To think that I should hear that mad thing sliding
    Along a smoking opal ladder!
Hear that inevitable deluge of music riding
    Into the sun, richer now — fainter now — madder!
To think that I should hear and know
The song that Shelley heard, and Shakespere, long ago!
Joseph Auslander

THE LARK

(Salisbury, England)

A CLOSE gray sky,
And poplars gray and high,
The country-side along;
The steeple bold
Across the acres old —
And then a song!

Oh, far, far, far,
As any spire or star,
Beyond the cloistered wall!
Oh, high, high, high,
A heart-throb in the sky —
Then not at all!

Lizette Woodworth Reese

A WORD WITH A SKYLARK

If this be all, for which I've listened long,
   Oh, spirit of the dew!
You did not sing to Shelley such a song
   As Shelley sang to you.

Yet with this ruined Old World for a nest,
   Worm-eaten through and through, —
This waste of grave-dust stamped with crown and crest, —
   What better could you do?

Ah, me! but when the world and I were young,
   There was an apple-tree,
There was a voice within the dawn that sung
   The buds awake — ah, me!

Oh, Lark of Europe, downward fluttering near,
   Like some spent leaf at best,
You'd never sing again if you could hear
   My Bluebird of the West!

Sarah M. B. Piatt

LARK'S SONG

In Mercer Street the light slants down,
And straightway an enchanted town
Is round him, pinnacle and spire
Flash back, elate, the sudden fire;
And clear above the silent street
Falls suddenly and strangely sweet
The lark's song. Bubbling, note on note
Rise fountain-like, o'erflow and float

Tide upon tide, and make more fair
The magic of the sunlit air.
No more the cage can do him wrong,
All is forgotten save his song:
He has forgot the ways of men,
Wide heaven is over him again,
And round him the wide fields of dew
That his first infant mornings knew,
Ere yet the dolorous years had brought
The hours of captive anguish, fraught
With the vile clamour of the street,
The insult of the passing feet,
The torture of the daily round,
The organ's blasphemy of sound.
Sudden some old swift memory brings
The knowledge of forgotten wings,
He springs elate and panting falls
At the rude touch of prison walls.
Silence. Again the street is grey;
Shut down the windows. Work-a-day.
Seumas O'Sullivan

From THE LARK ASCENDING

For, singing till his heaven fills,
'Tis love of earth that he instils,
And ever winging up and up,
Our valley is his golden cup,
And he the wine which overflows
To lift us with him as he goes:
The woods and brooks, the sheep and kine,
He is, the hills, the human line,
The meadows green, the fallows brown,
The dreams of labour in the town;

He sings the sap, the quickened veins;
The wedding song of sun and rains
He is, the dance of children, thanks
Of sowers, shout of primrose banks,
And eye of violets while they breathe;
All these the circling song will wreathe,
And you shall hear the herb and tree,
The better heart of men shall see,
Shall feel celestially, as long
As you crave nothing save the song.

George Meredith

A LATE LARK

A LATE lark twitters from the quiet skies;
And from the west,
Where the sun, his day's work ended,
Lingers as in content,
There falls on the old, gray city
An influence luminous and serene,
A shining peace.

The smoke ascends
In a rosy-and-golden haze. The spires
Shine, and are changed. In the valley
Shadows rise. The lark sings on. The sun,
Closing his benediction,
Sinks, and the darkening air
Thrills with a sense of the triumphing night —
Night with her train of stars
And her great gift of sleep.

So be my passing!
My task accomplished and the long day done,

My wages taken, and in my heart
Some late lark singing,
Let me be gathered to the quiet west,
The sundown splendid and serene,
Death.

William Ernest Henley

BLOW SOFTLY, THRUSH

Blow softly, thrush, upon the hush
That makes the least leaf loud,
Blow, wild of heart, remote, apart
From all the vocal crowd,
Apart, remote, a spirit note
That dances meltingly afloat,
Blow faintly, thrush!
And build the green-hid waterfall
I hated for its beauty, and all
The unloved vernal rapture and hush,
The old forgotten lonely time,
Delicate thrush!
Spring's at the prime, the world's in chime,
And my love is listening nearly;
O lightly blow the ancient woe,
Flute of the wood, blow clearly!
Blow, she is here, and the world all dear,
Melting flute of the hush,
Old sorrow estranged, enriched, sea-changed,
Breathe it, veery thrush!

Joseph Russell Taylor

THE VEERY

The moonbeams over Arno's vale in silvery flood were
    pouring,
When first I heard the nightingale a long-lost love
    deploring.
So passionate, so full of pain, it sounded strange and
    eerie;
I longed to hear a simpler strain, — the wood-notes of
    the veery.

The laverock sings a bonny lay above the Scottish
    heather;
It sprinkles down from far away like light and love
    together;
He drops the golden notes to greet his brooding mate,
    his dearie;
I only know one song more sweet, — the vespers of the
    veery.

In English gardens green and bright and full of fruity
    treasure,
I heard the blackbird with delight repeat his merry
    measure:
The ballad was a pleasant one, the tune was loud and
    cheery,
And yet with every setting sun I listened for the veery.

But far away, and far away, the tawny thrush is sing-
    ing;
New England woods, at close of day, with that clear
    chant are ringing:
And when my light of life is low, and heart and flesh
    are weary,
I fain would hear, before I go, the wood-notes of the
    veery.

Henry van Dyke

THRUSHES

Through Tanglewood the thrushes trip,
As brown as any clod,
But in their spotted throats are hung
The vesper-bells of God.

And I know little secret truths,
And hidden things of good,
Since I have heard the thrushes sing
At dusk, in Tanglewood.

Karle Wilson Baker

WOOD SONG

I heard a wood-thrush in the dusk
    Twirl three notes and make a star —
My heart that walked with bitterness
    Came back from very far.

Three shining notes were all he had,
    And yet they made a starry call —
I caught life back against my breast
    And kissed it, scars and all.

Sara Teasdale

WOOD-THRUSH

My brave,
You of the golden stave,
Though hidden, secret, furtive, still my brave,
You marshal me
Down aisles of ecstasy
Under Arcturus and the Pleiades.

With trill and run
(Apollo and bold Marsyas in one)
I am led on and on
Beyond all purples ever twilight wore
To the enchanted shore
Of dim and distant seas
That only dreamer's eyes have gazed upon.

Not all the invisible flutes of morn,
Not Memnon, newly born,
Crying against the ascendant torch of day,
Can match my minstrel — nay!
You, then, who crave
The fountain of pure music, spare delay,
And hasten down the dusky dew-cool way
To listen to my brave!
Clinton Scollard

ARTICULATE THRUSH

Oh, you and I, wild thrush — we share
   The glory of this mountain slope:
Its hallowed dusk, its fragrant air,
   Its haze of heliotrope.

We know the sweet tranquillity
   Of coming night: of the cool blue star,
The far jang-jangling bells from the lee
   Of the hills where the cattle are.

Not mine, but yours, the power to make
   Articulate the prayer that wells
In every heart this hour, the ache
   Of beauty in these dells.

Chant then, O bird, tilt back your bill;
  And, perched upon the balsam's nodding cones,
From out the plum-blue shadows spill
  Your pebbly silver tones.

Speak to whatever Cosmic Power
  Conjured to surging ecstasy
This day, its fire and dew and flower;
  And speak, sweet bird, for me.
                                Lew Sarett

THE WOOD-THRUSH

When lilies by the river fill with sun,
And banks with clematis are overrun;
When winds are weighed with fern-sweet from the hill,
And hawks wheel in the noontide hot and still;
When thistle-tops are silvered, every one,
And fly-lamps flicker ere the day is done,
Nature bethinks her how to crown these things,—
At twilight she decides: the wood-thrush sings.
                                John Vance Cheney

THE THRUSH

God bade the birds break not the silent spell
  That lay upon the wood.
Longing for liquid notes that never fell
  Ached the deep solitude.

The little birds obeyed. No voice awoke.
  Dwelling sedate, apart,

Only the thrush, the thrush that never spoke,
   Sang from her bursting heart.
Laura Benét

A THRUSH IN THE MOONLIGHT

IN came the moon and covered me with wonder,
Touched me and was near me and made me very still.
In came a rush of song, like rain after thunder,
Pouring importunate on my window-sill.

I lowered my head, I hid it, I would not see nor hear,
The birdsong had stricken me, had brought the moon too near.
But when I dared to lift my head, night began to fill
With singing in the darkness. And then the thrush grew still.
And the moon came, and silence, on my window-sill.
Witter Bynner

THE WISE THRUSH [1]

AND after April, when May follows,
And the whitethroat builds, and all the swallows —
Hark! where my blossomed pear-tree in the hedge
   Leans to the field and scatters on the clover
Blossoms and dewdrops — at the bent spray's edge —
   That's the wise thrush; he sings each song twice over,
Lest you should think he never could recapture
The first fine careless rapture!
Robert Browning

[1] The songs of the English thrushes differ markedly from those of the American.

BALLADE OF THE THRUSH

Across the noisy street
  I hear him careless throw
One warning utterance sweet;
  Then faint at first, and low,
  The full notes closer grow;
Hark! what a torrent gush!
  They pour, they overflow —
Sing on, sing on, O Thrush!

What trick, what dream's deceit,
  Has fooled his fancy so
To scorn of dust and heat?
  I, prisoned here below,
  Feel the fresh breezes blow;
And see, through flag and rush,
  Cool water sliding slow —
Sing on, sing on, O Thrush!

Sing on. What though thou beat
  On that dull bar, thy foe!
Somewhere the green boughs meet
  Beyond the roofs a-row;
  Somewhere the blue skies show,
Somewhere no black walls crush
  Poor hearts with hopeless woe —
Sing on, sing on, O Thrush!

ENVOY

Bird, though they come, we know,
  The empty cage, the hush;
Still, ere the brief days go,
  Sing on, sing on, O Thrush!

Austin Dobson

MY THRUSH

All through the sultry hours of June,
From morning blithe to golden noon,
  And till the star of evening climbs
The gray-blue east, a world too soon,
  There sings a thrush amid the limes.

God's poet, hid in foliage green,
Sings endless songs, himself unseen;
  Right seldom come his silent times.
Linger, ye summer hours serene!
  Sing on, dear thrush, amid the limes!

. . . .

May I not dream God sends thee there,
Thou mellow angel of the air,
  Even to rebuke my earthlier rhymes
With music's soul, all praise and prayer?
  Is that thy lesson in the limes?

Closer to God art thou than I:
His minstrel thou, whose brown wings fly
  Through silent ether's summer climes.
Ah, never may thy music die!
  Sing on, dear thrush, amid the limes!
              Mortimer Collins

A THRUSH BEFORE DAWN

A voice peals in this end of night
  A phrase of notes resembling stars,
Single and spiritual notes of light.
  What call they at my window-bars?
    The South, the past, the day to be,
    An ancient infelicity.

Darkling, deliberate, what sings
　　This wonderful one, alone, at peace?
What wilder things than song, what things
　　Sweeter than youth, clearer than Greece,
　　　　Dearer than Italy, untold
　　　　Delight, and freshness centuries old?

And first first-loves, a multitude,
　　The exaltation of their pain;
Ancestral childhood long renewed;
　　And midnights of invisible rain;
　　　　And gardens, gardens, night and day,
　　　　Gardens and childhood all the way.

What Middle Ages passionate,
　　O passionless voice! What distant bells
Lodged in the hills, what palace state
　　Illyrian! For it speaks, it tells,
　　　　Without desire, without dismay,
　　　　Some morrow and some yesterday.

All — natural things! But more — whence came
　　This yet remoter mystery?
How do these starry notes proclaim
　　A graver still divinity?
　　　　This hope, this sanctity of fear?
　　　　O innocent throat! O human ear!

　　　　　　　　　　　　Alice Meynell

THE DARKLING THRUSH

I LEANT upon a coppice gate
　　When Frost was spectre-gray,
The Winter's dregs made desolate
　　The weakening eye of day.

THE DARKLING THRUSH

The tangled bine-stems scored the sky
   Like strings of broken lyres,
And all mankind that haunted nigh
   Had sought their household fires.

The land's sharp features seemed to be
   The Century's corpse outleant,
His crypt the cloudy canopy,
   The wind his death-lament.
The ancient pulse of germ and birth
   Was shrunken hard and dry,
And every spirit upon earth
   Seemed feverless as I.

At once a voice arose among
   The bleak twigs overhead
In a full-hearted evensong
   Of joy illimited;
An aged thrush, frail, gaunt, and small,
   In blast-beruffled plume,
Had chosen thus to fling his soul
   Upon the growing gloom.

So little cause for carollings
   Of such ecstatic sound
Was written on terrestrial things
   Afar or nigh around,
That I could think there trembled through
   His happy good-night air
Some blessed Hope, whereof he knew
   And I was unaware.

Thomas Hardy

THE SONG OF THE HERMIT THRUSH

    From Casco Bay
       To Farallon
    No singer may
       One come upon
    In the woodland hush
    Save the hermit thrush
       With throat so like
    A carillon.
       There! Hear him strike
    A carillon!

    Changes he rings
       The same through the ages;
    Liltingly sings
       (We're told by the sages)
    One perfect theme
       Full a million years old
    When parvenu man
       First intruded the wold.

    Passionate pleader
       Of pleasure and pain,
    He is no heeder
       Of bluster or rain;
    Floating the stream
       Of a past everliving,
    Singing a lay
       For the sake of the singing,
    Giving love's gift
       For the sake of the giving,
    These are the changeless
       Changes he's ringing:

"Pebbles of gold
Dropped in a pool
   Of pine-girt silences,
Slowly unfold
Ripples of cool
   And liquid cadences."

From Casco Bay
   To Farallon
No singer may
   One come upon
In the woodland hush
Save the hermit thrush
   With throat so like
A carillon.
   There! Hear him strike
A carillon!

James B. Thomas

A HERMIT THRUSH IN THE CATSKILLS

"O spheral, spheral!" he seems to say;
"O holy, holy! Clear away, clear away!
"O clear up, clear up!" [1]

Harken the song of the thrush,
   Lulling the leaves to find
An aspen way to hush
   The far cry of the blind.

The forest has ever the stare
   Of something in the dark
That wonders where, O where
   Shall the arrow reach the mark.

[1] These lines are from John Burroughs's *Wake-Robin*.

Heart, but the arrow is keen
   That seeks the fawn and doe,
Is lethal, lithe and lean
   And swift to leave the bow...

Feathery trills and preludes
   Are a-quiver in the gloom
Of the ancestral woods
   That deepen like a tomb.

The Catskills shoulder the moon,
   And the stars are in flight.
Breaking, the day will soon
   Break the heart of the night.

Soon shall the buzzard and ant
   Be busy, and the owl
Be abashed by the chant
   Of the first barnyard fowl.

"O spheral, spheral!" hear him repeat;
"O holy, holy! Clear away, clear away!
"O clear up, clear up! Make it sweet!"
                             William Griffith

THE NIGHTINGALE

As it fell upon a day
In the merry month of May,
Sitting in a pleasant shade
Which a grove of myrtles made,
Beasts did leap and birds did sing,
Trees did grow and plants did spring;

Everything did banish moan
Save the Nightingale alone:
She, poor bird, as all forlorn,
Leaned her breast up-till a thorn,
And there sang the dolefull'st ditty
That to hear it was great pity.
Fie, fie, fie! now would she cry;
Tereu, tereu! by and by;
That to hear her so complain
Scarce I could from tears refrain;
For her griefs so lively shown
Made me think upon mine own.
Ah! thought I, thou mourn'st in vain,
None takes pity on thy pain:
Senseless trees they cannot hear thee;
Ruthless beasts they will not cheer thee:
King Pandion he is dead,
All thy friends are lapped in lead;
All thy fellow birds do sing
Careless of thy sorrowing:
Even so, poor bird, like thee
None alive will pity me.

Richard Barnfield

TO THE NIGHTINGALE

O NIGHTINGALE that on yon bloomy spray
Warblest at eve, when all the woods are still,
Thou with fresh hope the lover's heart dost fill,
While the jolly hours lead on propitious May.
Thy liquid notes that close the eye of day,
First heard before the shallow cuckoo's bill,
Portend success in love. O if Jove's will

Have linked that amorous power to thy soft lay,
Now timely sing, ere the rude bird of hate
Foretell my hopeless doom, in some grove nigh;
As thou from year to year hast sung too late
For my relief, yet hadst no reason why.
Whether the Muse or Love call thee his mate,
Both them I serve, and of their train am I.

John Milton

ODE TO A NIGHTINGALE

MY heart aches, and a drowsy numbness pains
   My sense, as though of hemlock I had drunk,
Or emptied some dull opiate to the drains
   One minute past, and Lethe-wards had sunk:
'Tis not through envy of thy happy lot,
   But being too happy in thy happiness, —
     That thou, light-wingèd Dryad of the trees,
       In some melodious plot
   Of beechen green, and shadows numberless,
     Singest of summer in full-throated ease.

O for a draught of vintage, that hath been
   Cooled a long age in the deep-delvèd earth,
Tasting of Flora and the country green,
   Dance, and Provençal song, and sunburnt mirth!
O for a beaker full of the warm South,
   Full of the true, the blushful Hippocrene,
     With beaded bubbles winking at the brim,
       And purple-stainèd mouth;
   That I might drink, and leave the world unseen,
     And with thee fade away into the forest dim:

ODE TO A NIGHTINGALE

Fade far away, dissolve, and quite forget
  What thou among the leaves hast never known,
The weariness, the fever, and the fret,
  Here, where men sit and hear each other groan;
Where palsy shakes a few, sad, last gray hairs,
  Where youth grows pale, and specter-thin, and dies;
    Where but to think is to be full of sorrow
      And leaden-eyed despairs;
  Where Beauty cannot keep her lustrous eyes,
    Or new Love pine at them beyond to-morrow.

Away! away! for I will fly to thee,
  Not charioted by Bacchus and his pards,
But on the viewless wings of Poesy,
  Though the dull brain perplexes and retards:
Already with thee! tender is the night,
  And haply the Queen-Moon is on her throne,
    Clustered around by all her starry Fays;
      But here there is no light,
  Save what from heaven is with the breezes blown
    Through verdurous glooms and winding mossy ways.

I cannot see what flowers are at my feet,
  Nor what soft incense hangs upon the boughs,
But, in embalmèd darkness, guess each sweet
  Wherewith the seasonable month endows
The grass, the thicket, and the fruit-tree wild;
  White hawthorn, and the pastoral eglantine;
    Fast-fading violets covered up in leaves;
      And mid-May's eldest child,
  The coming musk-rose, full of dewy wine,
    The murmurous haunt of flies on summer eves.

ODE TO A NIGHTINGALE

Darkling I listen; and, for many a time
　I have been half in love with easeful Death,
Called him soft names in many a musèd rhyme,
　To take into the air my quiet breath;
Now more than ever seems it rich to die,
　To cease upon the midnight with no pain,
　　While thou art pouring forth thy soul abroad
　　　In such an ecstasy!
　Still wouldst thou sing, and I have ears in vain —
　　To thy high requiem become a clod.

Thou wast not born for death, immortal Bird!
　No hungry generations tread thee down;
The voice I hear this passing night was heard
　In ancient days by emperor and clown:
Perhaps the self-same song that found a path
　Through the sad heart of Ruth, when, sick for home,
　　She stood in tears amid the alien corn;
　　　The same that oft-times hath
　Charmed magic casements, opening on the foam
　　Of perilous seas, in faery lands forlorn.

Forlorn! the very word is like a bell
　To toll me back from thee to my sole self!
Adieu! the fancy cannot cheat so well
　As she is famed to do, deceiving elf.
Adieu! adieu! thy plaintive anthem fades
　Past the near meadows, over the still stream,
　　Up the hill-side; and now 'tis buried deep
　　　In the next valley-glades:
　Was it a vision, or a waking dream?
　　Fled is that music: — do I wake or sleep?

John Keats

PHILOMELA

Hark! ah, the nightingale —
The tawny-throated!
Hark, from that moonlit cedar what a burst!
What triumph! hark! — what pain!

O wanderer from a Grecian shore,
Still, after many years, in distant lands,
Still nourishing in thy bewildered brain
That wild, unquenched, deep-sunken, old-world
    pain —
Say, will it never heal?
And can this fragrant lawn
With its cool trees, and night,
And the sweet, tranquil Thames,
And moonshine, and the dew,
To thy racked heart and brain
Afford no balm?

Dost thou to-night behold,
Here, through the moonlight on this English grass,
The unfriendly palace in the Thracian wild?
Dost thou again peruse
With hot cheeks and seared eyes
The too clear web, and thy dumb sister's shame?
Dost thou once more essay
Thy flight, and feel come over thee,
Poor fugitive, the feathery change
Once more, and once more seem to make resound
With love and hate, triumph and agony,
Lone Daulis, and the high Cephissian vale?
Listen, Eugenia –

How thick the bursts come crowding through the
   leaves!
Again — thou hearest?
Eternal passion!
Eternal pain!

Matthew Arnold

O NIGHTINGALE! THOU SURELY ART

O NIGHTINGALE! thou surely art
A creature of a "fiery heart": —
These notes of thine — they pierce and pierce;
Tumultuous harmony and fierce!
Thou sing'st as if the god of wine
Had helped thee to a Valentine;
A song in mockery and despite
Of shades and dews and silent night,
And steady bliss, and all the loves
Now sleeping in these peaceful groves.

I heard a stock-dove sing or say
His homely tale, this very day;
His voice was buried among trees,
Yet to be come at by the breeze:
He did not cease, but cooed — and cooed;
And somewhat pensively he wooed:
He sang of love, with quiet blending,
Slow to begin, and never ending;
Of serious faith, and inward glee;
That was the song — the song for me!

William Wordsworth

NIGHTINGALES

Beautiful must be the mountains whence ye come,
And bright in the fruitful valleys the streams wherefrom
　Ye learn your song:
Where are those starry woods? O might I wander there,
Among the flowers, which in that heavenly air
　Bloom the year long!

Nay, barren are those mountains and spent the streams:
Our song is the voice of desire, that haunts our dreams,
　A throe of the heart,
Whose pining visions dim, forbidden hopes profound,
No dying cadence nor long sigh can sound,
　For all our art.

Alone, aloud in the raptured ear of men
We pour our dark nocturnal secret; and then,
　As night is withdrawn
From these sweet-springing meads and bursting boughs of May,
Dream, while the innumerable choir of day
　Welcome the dawn.

Robert Bridges

FAIRFORD NIGHTINGALES

The nightingales at Fairford sing
As though it were a common thing
To make the day melodious
With tones that use to visit us

Only when thrush and blackbird take
Their sleep nor know the moon's awake.

These nightingales they sing at noon,
Not lyric lone, but threading June
With songs of many nightingales,
Till the meridian summer pales,
And here by day that spectral will
Is spending its enchantment still.

Nor shyly in far woodland bowers,
But walled among the garden flowers,
The Fairford nightingales are free,
That so the fabled melody
Is from the haunted groves of Thrace
Falling on Fairford market-place.

O nightingales that leave the night
To join the melodists of light,
And leave your coppiced gloom to dare
The fellowship forsaken there,
Fresh hours, fresh leaves can dispossess
Nor spoil your music's loneliness.
John Drinkwater

A DAMASCUS NIGHTINGALE

On the crimson edge of the eve,
  By the Barada's flute-like flow,
When the shadow-shuttles began to weave
  And the mountain airs to blow,
With sight of the eve's first star,
  As though it were dumb too long,

There burst on the ear a wondrous bar
  From a spirit dowered with song.

And I knew it for God's own bird,
  A prophet voice in the dark;
The budding stars in the heaven heard
  For they could not choose but hark.
Then the worn earth hid its face
  And dreamed its dream of the dawn;
The voice of man was stilled for a space,
  But the bird sang on and on.

Stephen Crombie

THE NIGHTINGALE UNHEARD

Yes, Nightingale, through all the summer-time
  We followed on, from moon to golden moon;
  From where Salerno day-dreams in the noon,
And the far rose of Pæstum once did climb.
  All the white way beside the girdling blue,
Through sun-shrill vines and campanile chime,
  We listened; — from the old year to the new.
    Brown bird, and where were you?

You, that Ravello lured not, throned on high
  And filled with singing out of sun-burned throats!
  Nor yet Minore of the flame-sailed boats;
Nor yet — of all bird-song should glorify —
  Assisi, Little Portion of the blest,
Assisi, in the bosom of the sky,
  Where God's own singer thatched his sunward nest;
    That little, heavenliest!

And north and north, to where the hedge-rows are,
  That beckon with white looks an endless way;
  Where, through the fair wet silverness of May,
A lamb shines out as sudden as a star,
  Among the cloudy sheep; and green, and pale,
The may-trees reach and glimmer, near or far,
  And the red may-trees wear a shining veil.
    And still no nightingale!

The one vain longing, — through all journeyings,
  The one: in every hushed and hearkening spot, —
  All the soft-swarming dark where you were not,
Still longed for! Yes, for sake of dreams and wings,
  And wonders, that your own must ever make
To bower you close, with all hearts' treasurings;
  And for that speech toward which all hearts do ache; —
    Even for Music's sake.

But most, his music whose belovèd name
  Forever writ in water of bright tears,
  Wins to one grave-side even the Roman years,
That kindle there the hallowed April flame
  Of comfort-breathing violets. By that shrine
Of Youth, Love, Death, forevermore the same,
  Violets still! — When falls, to leave no sign,
    The arch of Constantine.

Most for his sake we dreamed. Though not as he,
  From that lone spirit, brimmed with human woe,
  Your song once shook to surging overflow.
How was it, sovran dweller of the tree,
  His cry, still throbbing in the flooded shell
Of silence with remembered melody,

Could draw from you no answer to the spell?
— O Voice, O Philomel?

Long time we wondered (and we knew not why): —
  Nor dream, nor prayer, of wayside gladness born,
  Nor vineyards waiting, nor reproachful thorn,
Nor yet the nested hill-towns set so high
  All the white way beside the girdling blue, —
Nor olives gray against a golden sky,
  Could serve to wake that rapturous voice of you!
    But the wise silence knew.

O Nightingale unheard! — Unheard alone,
  Throughout that woven music of the days
  From the faint sea-rim to the market-place,
And ring of hammers on cathedral stone!
  So be it, better so: that there should fail
For sun-filled ones, one blessèd thing unknown.
  To them, be hid forever, — and all hail!
    Sing never, Nightingale.

Sing, for the others! Sing, to some pale cheek
  Against the window, like a starving flower.
  Loose, with your singing, one poor pilgrim hour
Of journey, with some Heart's Desire to seek.
  Loose, with your singing, captives such as these
In misery and iron, hearts too meek
  For voyage — voyage over dreamful seas
    To lost Hesperides.

Sing not for free-men. Ah, but sing for whom
  The walls shut in; and even as eyes that fade,
  The windows take no heed of light nor shade, —
The leaves are lost in mutterings of the loom.

THE NIGHTINGALE UNHEARD

Sing near! So in that golden overflowing
They may forget their wasted human bloom;
  Pay the devouring days their all, unknowing, —
    Reck not of life's bright going!

Sing not for lovers, side by side that hark;
  Nor unto parted lovers, save they be
  Parted indeed by more than makes the sea,
Where never hope shall meet — like mounting lark —
  Far Joy's uprising; and no memories
Abide to star the music-haunted dark:
  To them that sit in darkness, such as these,
    Pour down, pour down heart's-ease.

Not in King's gardens. No; but where there haunt
  The world's forgotten, both of men and birds;
  The alleys of no hope and of no words,
The hidings where men reap not, though they plant;
  But toil and thirst — so dying and so born; —
And toil and thirst to gather to their want,
  From the lean waste, beyond the daylight's scorn,
    — To gather grapes of thorn!

. . . .

And for those two, your pilgrims without tears,
  Who prayed a largess where there was no dearth,
  Forgive it them, brown music of the Earth:
Forgive it to their human-happy ears,
  Unknowing, — though the wiser silence knew!
Forgive it to the music of the spheres
  That while they walked together so, the Two
    Together, — heard not you.

Josephine Preston Peabody

THE SUMMER CHOIR

*"There will come the whitethroat's cry,
    That far lonely silver strain,
Piercing, like a sweet desire,
    The seclusion of the rain."*

THE WHITE-THROAT

The singing white-throat poured my gladness out,
And spread my golden wonder through the trees,
That day when Love burned the dead leaves of doubt,
And sifted sorrow's ashes to the breeze,
My soul sat in her sunshine by the door,
While her sweet spokesman told it o'er and o'er.
Anonymous

THE OVEN-BIRD

There is a singer everyone has heard,
Loud, a mid-summer and a mid-wood bird,
Who makes the solid tree trunks sound again.
He says that leaves are old and that for flowers
Mid-summer is to spring as one to ten.
He says the early petal-fall is past
When pears and cherry bloom went down in showers
On sunny days a moment overcast;
And comes that other fall we name the fall.
He says the highway dust is over all.
The bird would cease and be as other birds
But that he knows in singing not to sing.
The question that he frames in all but words
Is what to make of a diminished thing.
Robert Frost

THE LINNET

Upon this leafy bush
    With thorns and roses in it,
Flutters a thing of light,
    A twittering linnet,

And all the throbbing world
   Of dew and sun and air
By this small parcel of life
   Is made more fair;
As if each bramble-spray
   And mounded gold-wreathed furze,
Harebell and little thyme,
   Were only hers;
As if this beauty and grace
   Did to one bird belong,
And, as a flutter of wing,
   Might vanish in song.

Walter de la Mare

TO A BLUE TIT

Day after day you who are as free as air
(And how much freer, then, than I)
Venture your birthright, dare
That heavenly liberty, to fly
And feed upon my hand: I marvel why.

No other bird of your bright company
Commits a folly so divine!
Their chatter bids you be
Wary of guile — of some design
That you alone are conscious is not mine.

And even I, with less to lose than you,
I, wingless prisoner of the dust,
Would shun risks you renew
Each morning, not because you must,
But in a sweet wild miracle of trust.

Bird, as you call me to the window-ledge
With flashes and blue flutterings,
It seems the grey world's edge;
And, with the thrill your light touch brings,
I am your kin and know the lift of wings.
V. H. Friedlaender

BOB WHITE

Look! the valleys are thick with grain
    Heavy and tall;
Peaches drop in the heavy lane
    By the orchard wall;
Apples, streaked with a crimson stain,
    Bask in the sunshine, warm and bright:
Hark to the quail that pipes for rain —
    Bob White! Bob White!
Augur of mischief, pipes for rain —
    Bob White!

Men who reap on the fruitful plain
    Skirting the town,
Lift their eyes to the shifting vane
    As the sun goes down;
Slowly the farmer's loaded wain
    Climbs the slope in the failing light —
Bold is the voice that pipes for rain —
    Bob White! Bob White!
Still from the hillside, pipes for rain —
    Bob White!

Lo! a burst at the darkened pane,
    Angry and loud!
Waters murmur and winds complain
    To the rolling cloud;

Housed at the farm, the careless swain,
  Weaving snares while the fire burns bright,
Tuning his lips to the old refrain —
  Bob White! Bob White!
Oh, the sound of the blithe refrain —
  Bob White!

Dora Read Goodale

THE LAST BOB WHITE

Oh, how they murdered poor Bob White to-day!
  The booming guns were heard on every side,
From early morn till evening passed away
  The frightened coveys scattered far and wide.

No spot on earth could hide him from his foes
  For keen of scent the eager pointer came,
And flushed him from the ground, and as he rose
  He fell before the hunter's deadly aim.

But when the day was done, and all was still,
  And twilight's purple shades began to fall,
From off the summit of yon leafy hill
  I heard the echo of a lonely call.

It called into the night, but all in vain,
  For none of all his feathered mates was there
To sound the call responsive back again,
  And come to meet him through the chill night air.

They say this wanton slaughter is not sin —
  That birds and beasts were made for man's delight;
But oh! there is such lonely sadness in
  The plaintive calling of the last Bob White.

Whitney Montgomery

A MEADOW LARK SANG

A MEADOW lark sang at the drooping of dusk;
   Its silvery notes with the sea seemed in tune,
And out of the cloud like a blade from its sheath
   Night drew the new moon.

Then quenched in the dark was the lilt of the lark;
   The blade of the new moon was sheathed in the sea,
But the lips of the waves murmured still to the stars
   Impassionately.

Charles Commerford

BERCEUSE FOR BIRDS

Now that the twilight slants the curled edges of wheat
   And the bats go about amazed with dusk,
And there is the slurring sound of furry feet
   Where wheat ear chafes wheat ear, husk rubs husk —
And the noise of them is sweet;

Now that wind shadow moves in a devious arc
   Through fluttering blue flags, willow colonies;
And the nest-hovering little meadow lark
   Is hushed with numerous anxieties;
   And there is bronze rumor of bees, —

Slowly, with eyes withdrawn and intricate,
   Sleep of the moon-soft eyes, advancing slow,
Sleep, interceding and compassionate,
   Sway the mother lark's eyelids to forego
   Vigil: touch her so.

Joseph Auslander

PHŒBE [1]

It is a wee, sad-colored thing,
    As shy and secret as a maid,
That, ere in choir the robins sing,
    Pipes its own name, like one afraid.

It seems pain-prompted to repeat
    The story of some ancient ill,
But "Phœbe! Phœbe!" sadly sweet
    Is all it says, and then is still.

It calls, and listens. Earth and sky,
    Hushed by the pathos of its fate,
Listen; no whisper of reply
    Comes from its doom-dissevered mate.

"Phœbe!" is all it has to say
    In plaintive cadence o'er and o'er,
Like children who have lost their way,
    And know their names, and nothing more.
Anonymous

TO A PHŒBE BIRD

Under the eaves, out of the wet,
    You nest within my reach;
You never sing for me and yet
    You have a golden speech.

You sit and quirk a rapid tail,
    Wrinkle a ragged crest,

---

[1] The author of this poem has apparently confused the song of the chickadee with that of the phœbe.

You pirouette from tree to rail
    And vault from rail to nest.

And when in frequent dainty fright
    You gaily slip and fade,
And when at hand you re-alight
    Demure and unafraid,

And when you bring your brood its fill
    Of iridescent wings
And green legs dewy in your bill,
    Your silence is what sings.

Not a feather that enjoys
    To prate or praise or preach,
O Phœbe, with so little noise,
    What eloquence you teach!
Witter Bynner

GOLDFINCHES

Now that the giant sunflowers rise
    Along the garden way,
The shy goldfinches, seeking seeds,
    Visit them through the day.

One fancies as one watches them
    And hears their low refrain,
That they are sunbeams changed to birds
    That seek the sun again.
Elisabeth Scollard

THE GOLDFINCH

Down from the sky on a sudden he drops
Into the mullein and juniper tops,
Flushed from his bath in the midsummer shine
Flooding the meadowland, drunk with the wine
Spilled from the urns of the blue, like a bold
Sky-buccaneer in his sable and gold.

Lightly he sways on the pendulous stem,
Vividly restless, a fluttering gem,
Then with a flash of bewildering wings
Dazzles away up and down, and he sings
Clear as a bell at each dip as he flies
Bounding along on the wave of the skies.

Sunlight and laughter, a wingèd desire,
Motion and melody married to fire,
Lighter than thistle-tuft borne on the wind,
Frailer than violets, how shall we find
Words that will match him, discover a name
Meet for this marvel, this lyrical flame?

How shall we fashion a rhythm to wing with him,
Find us a wonderful music to sing with him
Fine as his rapture is, free as the rollicking
Song that the harlequin drops in his frolicking
Dance through the summer sky, singing so merrily
High in the burning blue, winging so airily?

Odell Shepard

CANTICLE

Devoutly worshiping the oak,
    Wherein the barred owl stares,

The little feathered forest folk
　Are praying sleepy prayers:

Praying the summer to be long
　And drowsy to the end,
And daily full of sun and song,
　That broken hopes may mend:

Praying the golden age to stay
　Until the whip-poor-will
Appoints a windy moving day,
　And hurries from the hill.
William Griffith

THE BOBOLINK

(From *The Biglow Papers*)

June's bridesman, poet o' the year,
Gladness on wings, the bobolink, is here;
Half-hid in tip-top apple-blooms he swings,
Or climbs against the breeze with quiverin' wings,
Or, givin' way to't in a mock despair,
Runs down, a brook o' laughter, through the air.
James Russell Lowell

ROBERT OF LINCOLN

Merrily swinging on brier and weed,
　Near to the nest of his little dame,
Over the mountain-side or mead,
　Robert of Lincoln is telling his name:
　　Bob-o'-link, bob-o'-link,
　　Spink, spank, spink;

ROBERT OF LINCOLN

Snug and safe is that nest of ours,
Hidden among the summer flowers.
                      Chee, chee, chee.

Robert of Lincoln is gayly dressed,
  Wearing a bright black wedding-coat;
White are his shoulders and white his crest.
  Hear him call in his merry note:
    Bob-o'-link, bob-o'-link,
      Spink, spank, spink;
Look, what a nice new coat is mine,
Sure there was never a bird so fine.
                      Chee, chee, chee.

Robert of Lincoln's Quaker wife,
  Pretty and quiet, with plain brown wings,
Passing at home a patient life,
  Broods in the grass while her husband sings:
    Bob-o'-link, bob-o'-link,
      Spink, spank, spink;
Brood, kind creature, you need not fear
Thieves and robbers while I am here.
                      Chee, chee, chee.

Modest and shy as a nun is she;
  One weak chirp is her only note.
Braggart and prince of braggarts is he,
  Pouring boasts from his little throat:
    Bob-o'-link, bob-o'-link,
      Spink, spank, spink;
Never was I afraid of man;
Catch me, cowardly knaves, if you can!
                      Chee, chee, chee.

ROBERT OF LINCOLN

Six white eggs on a bed of hay,
  Flecked with purple, a pretty sight!
There as the mother sits all day,
  Robert is singing with all his might:
    Bob-o'-link, bob-o'-link,
    Spink, spank, spink;
Nice good wife, that never goes out,
Keeping house while I frolic about.
                Chee, chee, chee.

Soon as the little ones chip the shell,
  Six wide mouths are open for food;
Robert of Lincoln bestirs him well,
  Gathering seeds for the hungry brood.
    Bob-o'-link, bob-o'-link,
    Spink, spank, spink;
This new life is likely to be
Hard for a gay young fellow like me.
                Chee, chee, chee.

Robert of Lincoln at length is made
  Sober with work, and silent with care;
Off his holiday garment laid,
  Half forgotten that merry air:
    Bob-o'-link, bob-o'-link,
    Spink, spank, spink;
Nobody knows but my mate and I
Where our nest and our nestlings lie.
                Chee, chee, chee.

Summer wanes; the children are grown;
  Fun and frolic no more he knows;
Robert of Lincoln's a humdrum crone;
  Off he flies, and we sing as he goes:

Bob-o'-link, bob-o'-link,
Spink, spank, spink;
When you can pipe that merry old strain,
Robert of Lincoln, come back again.
Chee, chee, chee.
William Cullen Bryant

TO THE LAPLAND LONGSPUR

Oh, thou northland bobolink,
Looking over Summer's brink
Up to Winter, worn and dim,
Peering down from mountain rim,
Something takes me in thy note,
Quivering wing, and bubbling throat;
Something moves me in thy ways —
Bird, rejoicing in thy days,
In thy upward-hovering flight;
In thy suit of black and white,
Chestnut cape and circled crown,
In thy mate of speckled brown;
Surely I may pause and think
Of my boyhood's bobolink.

Soaring over meadows wild
(Greener pastures never smiled);
Raining music from above,
Full of rapture, full of love;
Frolic, gay and debonair,
Yet not all exempt from care,
For thy nest is in the grass,
And thou worriest as I pass:
But nor hand nor foot of mine
Shall do harm to thee or thine;

I, musing, only pause to think
Of my boyhood's bobolink.

But no bobolink of mine
Ever sang o'er mead so fine,
Starred with flowers of every hue,
Gold and purple, white and blue;
Painted cup, anemone,
Jacob's-ladder, fleur-de-lis,
Orchid, harebell, shooting-star,
Crane's-bill, lupine, seen afar,
Primrose, poppy, saxifrage,
Pictured type on Nature's page —
These and others here unnamed,
In northland gardens, yet untamed,
Deck the fields where thou dost sing,
Mounting up on trembling wing;
While in wistful mood I think
Of my boyhood's bobolink.

On Unaláska's emerald lea,
On lonely isles in Bering Sea,
On far Siberia's barren shore,
On north Alaska's tundra floor,
At morn, at noon, in pallid night,
We heard thy song and saw thy flight,
While I, sighing, could but think
Of my boyhood's bobolink.
John Burroughs

THE RAIN-CROW

Can freckled August, — drowsing warm and blonde
Beside a wheat-shock in the white-topped mead,

In her hot hair the ox-eyed daisies wound, —
  O bird of rain, lend aught but sleepy heed
  To thee? when no plumed weed, no feathered seed
Blows by her; and no ripple breaks the pond,
  That gleams like flint between its rim of grasses,
  Through which the dragonfly forever passes
    Like splintered diamond.

Drouth weights the trees, and from the farmhouse eaves
  The locust, pulse-beat of the summer day,
Throbs; and the lane, that shambles under leaves
  Limp with the heat — a league of rutty way —
  Is lost in dust; and sultry scents of hay
Breathe from the panting meadows heaped with sheaves.
  Now, now, O bird, what hint is there of rain,
  In thirsty heaven or on burning plain,
    That thy keen eye perceives?

But thou art right. Thou prophesiest true.
  For hardly hast thou ceased thy forecasting,
When, up the western fierceness of scorched blue,
  Great water-carrier winds their buckets bring
  Brimming with freshness. How their dippers ring
And flash and rumble! lavishing dark dew
  On corn and forestland, that streaming wet,
  Their hilly backs against the downpour set,
    Like giants vague in view.

The butterfly, safe under leaf and flower,
  Has found a roof, knowing how true thou art;
The bumble-bee, within the last half hour,
  Has ceased to hug the honey to its heart;

While in the barnyard, under shed and cart,
Brood-hens have housed. — But I, who scorned thy power,
Barometer of birds, — like August there, —
Beneath a beech, dripping from foot to hair,
   Like some drenched truant, cower.
                              Madison Cawein

MAGPIES IN PICARDY

The magpies in Picardy
Are more than I can tell.
They flicker down the dusty roads
And cast a magic spell
On the men who march through Picardy,
Through Picardy to Hell.

(The blackbird flies with panic,
The swallow goes like light,
The finches move like ladies,
The owl floats by at night;
But the great and flashing magpie
He flies as artists might.)

A magpie in Picardy
Told me secret things —
Of the music in white feathers,
And the sunlight that sings
And dances in deep shadows —
He told me with his wings.

(The hawk is cruel and rigid,
He watches from a height;

The rook is slow and sombre,
The robin loves to fight;
But the great and flashing magpie
He flies as lovers might.)

He told me that in Picardy,
An age ago or more,
While all his fathers still were eggs,
These dusty highways bore
Brown singing soldiers marching out
Through Picardy to war.

He said that still through chaos
Works on the ancient plan,
And two things have altered not
Since first the world began —
The beauty of the wild green earth
And the bravery of man.

(For the sparrow flies unthinking
And quarrels in his flight;
The heron trails his legs behind,
The lark goes out of sight;
But the great and flashing magpie
He flies as poets might.)

T. P. Cameron Wilson

WINGED JEWELS

*"Is it a gem, half bird,
    Or is it a bird, half gem?"*

TO AN ORIOLE

How falls it, oriole, thou hast come to fly
In tropic splendor through our northern sky?

At some glad moment was it Nature's choice
To dower a scrap of sunset with a voice?

Or did some orange tulip, flaked with black,
In some forgotten garden, ages back,

Yearning toward heaven until its wish was heard,
Desire unspeakably to be a bird?

Edgar Fawcett

SPRING'S TORCH-BEARER

ORIOLE — athlete of the air —
   Of fire and song a glowing core,
From tropic wildernesses fair,
   Spring's favorite lampadephore,

A hot flambeau on either wing
   Rimples as you pass me by;
'Tis seeing flame to hear you sing,
   'Tis hearing song to see you fly.

Below the leaves in fragrant gloom,
   Cool currents lead you to your goal,
Where bursting jugs of rich perfume
   Down honeyed slopes of verdure roll.

SPRING'S TORCH-BEARER

In eddies, round some hummock cold,
   Where violets weave their azure bredes,
You flash a torch o'er rimy mould
   And rouse the dormant balsam seeds.

Upon the sassafras a flare,
   And through the elm a wavering sheen,
A flicker in the orchard fair,
   A flame across the hedgerow green.

Your voice and light are in my dream
   Of vanished youth, they warm my heart;
With every chirrup, every gleam,
   Sweet currents from old fountains start.

I take me wings and fly with you,
   Once more the boy of long ago,
Oh, days of bloom! Oh, honey-dew!
   Hark! how the flutes of fairy blow!

You whisk wild splendors through the trees,
   And send keen fervors down the wind,
You singe the jackets of the bees,
   And trail an opal mist behind.

When flowery hints foresay the berry,
   On spray of haw and tuft of brier,
Then, wandering incendiary,
   You set the maple swamps afire!

Maurice Thompson

REDBIRDS

REDBIRDS, redbirds,
   Long and long ago,
What a honey-call you had
   In hills I used to know!

Redbud, buckberry,
   Wild plum-tree
And proud river sweeping
   Southward to the sea,

Brown and gold in the sun
   Sparkling far below,
Trailing stately round her bluffs
   Where the poplars grow —

Redbirds, redbirds,
   Are you singing still
As you sang one May day
   On Saxton's Hill?

Sara Teasdale

TO A SCARLET TANAGER

O SPARK, you winged from secret woodland forges
Where starry hammers beat a tune of dreams;
Their smoke hangs fragrant blue mist in the gorges,
Their pulse is throbbing wildly in the streams.
You are a presence from recurrent wonder
That patterns through the urge into the leaf.
On quivering flanks of the retreating thunder
Your notes turn banners, glorious and brief.

Brief like the rapture that this day uncloses,
O fitting song that sings long after still...
You show the path — we seek the wild new roses,
You hint of distance — and we climb the hill.
Against the woodland's haze your flaming breast!
You gave the clue and we must find the rest.

Glenn Ward Dresbach

THE SCARLET TANAGER

A BALL of fire shoots through the tamarack
In scarlet splendor, on voluptuous wings;
Delirious joy the pyrotechnist brings,
Who marks for us high summer's almanac.
How instantly the red-coat hurtles back!
No fiercer flame has flashed beneath the sky.
Note now the rapture in his cautious eye,
The conflagration lit along his track.
Winged soul of beauty, tropic in desire,
Thy love seems alien in our northern zone;
Thou givest to our green lands a burst of fire
And callest back the fables we disown.
The hot equator thou mightst well inspire,
Or stand above some Eastern monarch's throne.

Joel Benton

THE CARDINAL BIRD

(Extract)

A DAY and then a week passed by:
  The redbird hanging from the sill
Sang not; and all were wondering why
  It was so still —

THE CARDINAL BIRD

When one bright morning, loud and clear,
Its whistle smote my drowsy ear,
Ten times repeated, till the sound
Filled every echoing niche around;
And all things earliest loved by me, —
The bird, the brook, the flower, the tree, —
Came back again, as thus I heard
  The cardinal bird.

Where maple orchards towered aloft,
  And spicewood bushes spread below,
Where skies were blue, and winds were soft,
  I could but go —
For, opening through a wildering haze,
Appeared my restless childhood days;
And truant feet and loitering mood
Soon found me in the same old wood
(Illusion's hour but seldom brings
So much the very form of things)
When first I sought, and saw, and heard
  The cardinal bird.

Then came green meadows, broad and bright,
  Where dandelions, with wealth untold,
Gleamed on the young and eager sight
  Like stars of gold;
And on the very meadow's edge,
Beneath the ragged blackberry hedge,
Mid mosses golden, gray, and green,
The fresh young buttercups were seen,
And small spring-beauties, sent to be
The heralds of anemone:
All just as when I earliest heard
  The cardinal bird.

William Davis Gallagher

TO A GROSBEAK IN THE GARDEN

When through the heaviness and clamouring throng
Of mortal ways I hear the mellow song
Of birds, the birds seem sent to me.
If this be my insanity,
As men will measure it — so let it be!

When shadows that no will can drive away
Entomb me — then no sermon blesseth day
More true and sweet than that pure note
My ear hath caught afloat,
Aflame from the red-breast's fervent throat.

Thou, crimson-caped messenger of God,
Seem'st not to feel the thorned and bruising rod
Of Life — thy hours are joyously beguiled
With melody so mild,
So wild! — as winds in the heart of some slip-trammel child.

Full knowing that thy living days are brief
Thou grudgest even a breath for sober grief;
Thy poems are scattered free, without a name,
Nor hast thou thought of fame —
Neither from the eagle taken shame!
Is *my* unpaid aspiring yet my blame?

The world is wide 'twixt man and worlds divine,
And hearts are dull to such a song as thine;
But I have heard. Sing on, from tree to tree,
As thou hast sung to me —
And more shall find the God that guideth thee!

Ivan Swift

INDIGO BIRD

I WILL fare up White Creek Water
  Whose banks are green and mossy;
I will fare up White Creek Water
  Now the summer sun is high;
I will cut me a staff of hazel
  Where the leaves are thick and glossy,
And watch the twinkling trout-fin
  Where the current dimples by.

There will come a chirp from the thicket;
  I will crane my head to hear it —
    A queer call, a clear call, a cry;
A voice that is low and plaintive
  With something to endear it;
Then I will glimpse a vivid breast
  Like a little scrap of sky.

There by the White Creek Water
  Just the flicker of a feather,
    And a soft note from a throat of brilliant dye,
And then a golden silence
  In the dreamy summer weather
By the banks of the White Creek Water
  Where the current dimples by.

Stephen Crombie

HUMMING BIRD

It would take an angel's eye
  To see the humming bird's hot wings.
He stands raptly on thin air
  At his banquetings.

He flies so fast he is at rest,
   His vibrant body poises still,
His wings into the crystal light
   Melt invisible.

A bobbin winding off the threads
   Of sunlight from the spools of flowers,
His hunger is a weightless thing
   And holier than ours.

Saints and angels bathed in flame
   Know far less of flame than he
As he hovers pinionless
   A minute ecstasy.

Robert P. Tristram Coffin

THE HUMMING BIRD

A WINGED rocket curving through
   An amethystine airy sea,
Blew up the magazines of dew
   Within the fortress of the bee.

Some say the tulip mortar sent
   The missile forth — I do not know.
I scarcely saw which way it went
   The flash of flame surprised me so.

The bees forgot to sound alarm,
   And did not pause their gates to lock;
A topaz terror took by storm
   The tall tower of the hollyhock.

Around the rose a halo hung
  As if the bomb had been a gem,
And round the dahlia's head there swung
  A blade that looked a diadem.

What more befell I cannot say;
  The ruby glint and emerald gleam
So dazed my sense, the garden lay
  Around me like an opal dream.

Maurice Thompson

THE HUMMING BIRD

Dancer of air,
Flashing thy flight across the noontide hour,
To pierce and pass ere it is full aware
  Each wondering flower!

Jewelled coryphée,
With quivering wings like shielding gauze outspread,
And measure like a gleaming shuttle's play
  With unseen thread!

The phlox, milk-white,
Sways to thy whirling; stirs each warm rose breast;
But not for these thy palpitant delight,
  Thy rhythmic quest;

Swift weaves thy maze
Where flaunts the trumpet-vine its scarlet pride,
Where softer fire, behind its chaliced blaze,
  Doth fluttering hide.

A HUMMING BIRD

The grave thrush sings
His love-call, and the nightingale's romance
Throbs through the twilight; thou hast but thy wings,
    Thy sun-thrilled dance.

Yet doth love's glow
Burn in the ruby of thy restless throat,
Guiding thy voiceless ecstasy to know
    The richest note

Of brooding thrush!
Now for thy joy the emptied air doth long;
Thine is the nested silence, and the hush
    That needs no song.

Ednah Proctor Clarke

A HUMMING BIRD

WHEN the mild gold stars flower out,
    As the summer gloaming goes,
A dim shape quivers about
    Some sweet rich heart of a rose.

If you watch its fluttering poise,
    From palpitant wings will steal
A hum like the eerie noise
    Of an elfin spinning-wheel!

And then from the shape's vague sheen,
    Quick lustres of blue will float,
That melt in luminous green
    Round a glimmer of ruby throat!

But fleetly across the gloom
  This tremulous shape will dart,
While searching for some fresh bloom
  To quiver about its heart.

Then you, by thoughts of it stirred,
  Will dreamily question them;
"Is it a gem, half bird,
  Or is it a bird, half gem?"
Edgar Fawcett

THE HUMMING BIRD

When languorous noons entreat the summer sky,
  And restive spirits vex the ways of men
  In vain emprise; within my garden then
Will I elect to let the world go by,
And watch the humming bird. Not seen to fly,
  He comes and vanishes and comes again
  And sips the sweets of honeysuckles when
Their lips are frail — but leaves them not to die.

So I have thought how good it were to be
  This ruthful corsair, bent on such pursuit,
    Against the wear of my foreplanning hours; —
How good it were to live thus liegelessly
  Upon the world's unreckoned blossom-loot —
    Yet spare from any harm its guarded flowers!
Ivan Swift

MOCKERS

"Thou sportive satirist of Nature's school."

THE MOCKING BIRD

Hear! hear! hear!
Listen! the word
Of the mocking bird!
Hear! hear! hear!
I will make all clear;
I will let you know
Where the footfalls go
That through the thicket and over the hill
Allure, allure.
How the bird-voice cleaves
Through the weft of leaves
With a leap and a thrill
Like the flash of a weaver's shuttle, swift and
    sudden and sure!

And lo, he is gone — even while I turn
The wisdom of his runes to learn.
He knows the mystery of the wood,
The secret of the solitude;
But he will not tell, he will not tell,
For all he promises so well.

Richard Hovey

TO THE MOCKING BIRD

WINGED mimic of the woods! thou motley fool!
Who shall thy gay buffoonery describe?
Thine ever-ready notes of ridicule
Pursue thy fellows still with jest and gibe.
Wit, sophist, songster, Yorick of thy tribe,

Thou sportive satirist of Nature's school,
To thee the palm of scoffing we ascribe,
Arch-mocker and mad Abbot of Misrule!
For such thou art by day, — but all night long
Thou pourest a soft, sweet, pensive, solemn strain,
As if thou didst in this thy moonlight song
Like to the melancholy Jacques complain,
Musing on falsehood, folly, vice, and wrong,
And sighing for thy motley coat again.

Richard Henry Wilde

THE MOCKING BIRD

Lord of the odored alleys green! who on the silence flings
A rippling joy and laughter as from god-touched, golden strings,
Are you looking through the pearly gates? — The clock has struck eleven —
I think out there
In the moonlit air
You can hear the harps of heaven!

Translating beauty into sound, you weave the glad day long
Sun, moon and star and rainbow-gleams in a bridal robe of song.
And you dye with the blood of roses, as you spin on the airy looms,
And you dip the skein
From your teeming brain
In the scent of the orange blooms.

Deep down in a jasmine thicket, 'neath a tangle of gold and green,
She lives with her growing little ones in a home no man has seen.
I heard you there a-teaching school in a sly and secret way.
In a story-song,
Whispered and long,
You told of the sunlit day.

What tender love and heavenly joy were in the whispered notes!
I think it made them stir their wings and ruffle up their throats.
The magic things, beloved of God, by seers and poets sung
That lift the eyes
To Paradise
Are beauty and the young.

Irving Bacheller

THE MOCKING BIRD

Superb and sole, upon a plumèd spray
That o'er the general leafage boldly grew,
He summed the woods in song; or typic drew
The watch of hungry hawks, the lone dismay
Of languid doves when long their lovers stray,
And all birds' passion plays that sprinkle dew
At morn in brake or bosky avenue.
Whate'er birds did or dreamed, this bird could say.

Then down he shot, bounced airily along
The sward, twitched in a grasshopper, made song

Midflight, perched, prinked, and to his art again.
Sweet Science, this large riddle read me plain:
How may the death of that dull insect be
The life of yon trim Shakespere on the tree?

Sidney Lanier

THE FLUTE OF KRISHNA

No human lips caress,
Nor breath of man inspires,
The mystic flute
Vibrant amid the orange blooms
This night.
Instead,
Swaying in the full moon's
Lights and shades,
The instrument
Of the invisible Flutist
Plays itself.

What is this living flute?
The twin spirit of the nightingale
Amid Arabia's roses singing —
Awakening within the listener's soul
A song ineffable.

For in the stillness,
All the earthly sweetness
Of Life and Love and Death
Is trebled forth in living tones
By Krishna's flute —
The mocking bird.

James B. Thomas

TO A MOCKING BIRD

I

I WATCHED the day come up the road
With sunlight on her hair;
Her dancing feet were silver-shod
To make the dawn more fair.

When from a thicket deep and cool
I heard a mocking bird
Pour forth its welcome in a song
That angels might have heard.

II

I stood to bid the day good-night
As she with dusky feet
Stole down the pathway to the wood
Where all true lovers meet.

When from the shadows of the night
I heard the selfsame voice
Pour forth its bursting heart in song —
"Rejoice, oh, Day! rejoice!"

If only I might greet the Day,
Oh, mocking bird, as thou!
If only I might face the Dark
With song, as thou dost now!
Edwin Osgood Grover

OUT OF THE CRADLE ENDLESSLY ROCKING

I

Out of the cradle endlessly rocking,
Out of the mocking-bird's throat, the musical shuttle,
Out of the Ninth-month midnight,
Over the sterile sands, and the fields beyond, where the child, leaving his bed, wandered alone, bareheaded, barefoot,
Down from the showered halo,
Up from the mystic play of shadows, twining and twisting as if they were alive,
Out from the patches of briers and blackberries,
From the memories of the bird that chanted to me,
From your memories, sad brother — from the fitful risings and fallings I heard,
From under that yellow half-moon, late-risen, and swollen as if with tears,
From those beginning notes of sickness and love, there in the transparent mist,
From the thousand responses of my heart, never to cease,
From the myriad thence-aroused words,
From the word stronger and more delicious than any,
From such, as now they start, the scene revisiting,
As a flock, twittering, rising, or overhead passing,
Borne hither — ere all eludes me, hurriedly,
A man — yet by these tears a little boy again,
Throwing myself on the sand, confronting the waves,
I, chanter of pains and joys, uniter of here and hereafter,
Taking all hints to use them — but swiftly leaping beyond them,
A reminiscence sing.

II

Once, Paumanok,
When the snows had melted — when the lilac-scent
    was in the air, and the Fifth-month grass was
    growing,
Up this sea-shore, in some briers,
Two guests from Alabama — two together,
And their nest, and four light-green eggs, spotted with
    brown,
And every day the he-bird, to and fro, near at hand,
And every day the she-bird, crouched on her nest,
    silent, with bright eyes,
And every day I, a curious boy, never too close, never
    disturbing them,
Cautiously peering, absorbing, translating.

III

Shine! shine! shine!
Pour down your warmth, great Sun!
While we bask — we two together.

Two together!
Winds blow South, or winds blow North,
Day come white, or night come black,
Home, or rivers and mountains from home,
Singing all time, minding no time,
While we two keep together.

IV

Till of a sudden,
May-be killed, unknown to her mate,
One forenoon the she-bird crouched not on the nest,
Nor returned that afternoon, nor the next,
Nor ever appeared again.

And thenceforward, all summer, in the sound of the
    sea,
And at night, under the full of the moon, in calmer
    weather,
Over the hoarse surging of the sea,
Or flitting from brier to brier by day,
I saw, I heard at intervals, the remaining one, the he-
    bird,
The solitary guest from Alabama.

V

Blow! blow! blow!
Blow up, sea-winds, along Paumanok's shore!
I wait and I wait, till you blow my mate to me.

VI

Yes, when the stars glistened,
All night long, on the prong of a moss-scalloped stake,
Down, almost amid the slapping waves,
Sat the lone singer, wonderful, causing tears.

He called on his mate;
He poured forth the meanings which I, of all men,
    know.

Yes, my brother, I know;
The rest might not — but I have treasured every note;
For once, and more than once, dimly, down to the
    beach gliding,
Silent, avoiding the moonbeams, blending myself with
    the shadows,
Recalling now the obscure shapes, the echoes,
    the sounds and sights after their sorts,
The white arms out in the breakers tirelessly tossing,

OUT OF THE CRADLE

I, with bare feet, a child, the wind wafting my hair,
Listened long and long.

Listened, to keep, to sing — now translating the notes,
Following you, my brother.

VII

Soothe! soothe! soothe!
Close on its wave soothes the wave behind,
And again another behind, embracing and lapping, every
one close,
But my love soothes not me, not me.

Low hangs the moon — it rose late;
O it is lagging — O I think it is heavy with love, with love.

O madly the sea pushes, pushes upon the land,
With love — with love.

O night! do I not see my love fluttering out there among
the breakers?
What is that little black thing I see there in the white?

Loud! loud! loud!
Loud I call to you, my love!

High and clear I shoot my voice over the waves;
Surely you must know who is here, is here;
You must know who I am, my love.

Low-hanging moon!
What is that dusky spot in your brown yellow?
O it is the shape, the shape of my mate!
O moon, do not keep her from me any longer.

Land! land! O land!
Whichever way I turn, O I think you could give me my mate back again, if you only would;
For I am almost sure I see her dimly whichever way I look.

O rising stars!
Perhaps the one I want so much will rise, will rise with some of you.

O throat! O trembling throat!
Sound clearer through the atmosphere!
Pierce the woods, the earth;
Somewhere listening to catch you, must be the one I want.

Shake out, carols!
Solitary here — the night's carols!
Carols of lonesome love! Death's carols!
Carols under that lagging, yellow, waning moon!
O, under that moon, where she droops almost down into the sea!
O reckless, despairing carols.

But soft! sink low;
Soft! let me just murmur;
And do you wait a moment, you husky-noised sea;
For somewhere I believe I heard my mate responding to me,
So faint — I must be still, be still to listen;
But not altogether still, for then she might not come immediately to me.

Hither, my love!
Here I am! Here!

OUT OF THE CRADLE

With this just-sustained note I announce myself to you;
This gentle call is for you, my love, for you.

Do not be decoyed elsewhere!
That is the whistle of the wind — it is not my voice;
That is the fluttering, the fluttering of the spray;
Those are the shadows of leaves.

O darkness! O in vain!
O I am very sick and sorrowful.

O brown halo in the sky, near the moon, drooping upon the sea!
O troubled reflection in the sea!
O throat! O throbbing heart!
O all — and I singing uselessly, uselessly all the night.

Yet I murmur, murmur on!
O murmurs — you yourselves make me continue to sing, I know not why.

O past! O life! O songs of joy!
In the air — in the woods — over fields;
Loved! loved! loved! loved! loved!
But my love no more, no more with me!
We two together no more.

VIII

The aria sinking;
All else continuing — the stars shining,
The winds blowing — the notes of the bird continuous echoing,
With angry moans the fierce old mother incessantly moaning,

On the sands of Paumanok's shore, gray and rustling;
The yellow half-moon enlarged, sagging down, drooping, the face of the sea almost touching;
The boy extatic — with his bare feet the waves, with his hair the atmosphere dallying,
The love in the heart long pent, now loose, now at last tumultuously bursting,
The aria's meaning, the ears, the Soul, swiftly depositing,
The strange tears down the cheeks coursing,
The colloquy there — the trio — each uttering,
The undertone — the savage old mother, incessantly crying,
To the boy's Soul's questions sullenly timing — some drowned secret hissing,
To the outsetting bard of love.

IX

Demon or bird! (said the boy's soul,)
Is it indeed toward your mate you sing? or is it mostly to me?
For I, that was a child, my tongue's use sleeping,
Now I have heard you,
Now in a moment I know what I am for — I awake,
And already a thousand singers — a thousand songs, clearer, louder and more sorrowful than yours,
A thousand warbling echoes have started to life within me,
Never to die.

O you singer, solitary, singing by yourself — projecting me;
O solitary me, listening — nevermore shall I cease perpetuating you;

OUT OF THE CRADLE

Never more shall I escape, never more the reverberations,
Never more the cries of unsatisfied love be absent from me,
Never again leave me to be the peaceful child I was before what there, in the night,
By the sea, under the yellow and sagging moon,
The messenger there aroused — the fire, the sweet hell within,
The unknown want, the destiny of me.

O give me the clue! (it lurks in the night here somewhere;)
O if I am to have so much, let me have more!
O a word! O what is my destination? (I fear it is henceforth chaos;)
O how joys, dreads, convolutions, human shapes, and all shapes, spring as from graves around me!
O phantoms! you cover all the land and all the sea!
O I cannot see in the dimness whether you smile or frown upon me;
O vapor, a look, a word! O well-beloved!
O you dear women's and men's phantoms!
A word then, (for I will conquer it,)
The word final, superior to all,
Subtle, sent up — what is it? — I listen;
Are you whispering it, and have been all the time, you sea-waves?
Is that it from your liquid rims and wet sands?

X

Whereto answering, the sea,
Delaying not, hurrying not

Whispered me through the night, and very plainly before day-break,
Lisped to me the low and delicious word DEATH;
And again Death — ever Death, Death, Death,
Hissing melodious, neither like the bird, nor like my aroused child's heart,
But edging near, as privately for me, rustling at my feet,
Creeping thence steadily up to my ears, and laving me softly all over,
Death, Death, Death, Death, Death.

Which I do not forget,
But fuse the song of my dusky demon and brother,
That he sang to me in the moonlight on Paumanok's gray beach,
With the thousand responsive songs, at random,
My own songs, awaked from that hour;
And with them the key, the word up from the waves,
The word of the sweetest song, and all songs,
That strong and delicious word which, creeping to my feet,
The sea whispered me.

Walt Whitman

MY CATBIRD

(Extract)

NIGHTINGALE I never heard,
Nor skylark, poet's bird;
But there is an æther-winger
So surpasses every singer,
(Though unknown to lyric fame,)

That at morning, or at nooning,
When I hear his pipe a-tuning,
Down I fling Keats, Shelley, Wordsworth, —
What are all their songs of birds worth?
All their soaring
Souls' outpouring?
When my Mimus Carolinensis,
(That's his Latin name,)
When my warbler wild commences
Song's hilarious rhapsody,
Just to please himself and me!
Primo Cantante!
Scherzo! Andante!
Piano, pianissimo!
Presto, prestissimo!

William Henry Venable

CATBIRD

Who can be that somber fellow
Garbed in gray?
Is it Puck or Punchinello
Perched upon a birchen spray?
Eyes that gleam and eyes that glisten,
(Listen, listen,
While he runs his gamut through!)
He's the minstrel of the thicket,
Chirk and cheery as a cricket
Although clad in sober hue.

Spry — no fairy could be spryer —
As he tunes his airy lyre;
Merry, mellow avalanches
Toss and tumble from the branches;

All his trills and all his trebles,
Like a rillet over pebbles,
Have a lovely lyric lure;
He is tricksy
As a pixy,
This gay feathered troubadour.

Stephen Crombie

TO THE CATBIRD

You, who would with wanton art
Counterfeit another's part,
And with noisy utterance claim
Right to an ignoble name, —
Inharmonious! — why must you,
To a better self untrue,
Gifted with the charm of song,
Do the generous gift such wrong?

Delicate and downy throat,
Shaped for pure, melodious note,
Silvery wings of softest gray,
Bright eyes glancing every way,
Graceful outline, motion free —
Types of perfect harmony!

Ah! you much mistake your duty,
Mating discord thus with beauty, —
'Mid these heavenly sunset gleams,
Vexing the smooth air with screams, —
Burdening the dainty breeze
With insane discordancies.

I have heard you tell a tale
Tender as the nightingale,

TO THE CATBIRD

Sweeter than the early thrush
Pipes at day-dawn from the bush.
Wake once more the liquid strain
That you poured, like music-rain,
When, last night, in the sweet weather,
You and I were out together.

Unto whom two notes are given,
One of earth, and one of heaven,
Were it not a shameful tale
That the earth-note should prevail?

For the sake of those who love us,
For the sake of God above us,
Each and all should do their best
To make music for the rest.

So I will no more reprove,
Though the chiding be in love:
Uttering harsh rebuke to you,
That were inharmonious, too.

Anonymous

THE LESSER CHILDREN

"Watchmen of whom our safety takes no heed."

THE LESSER CHILDREN

A THRENODY AT THE HUNTING SEASON

In the middle of August when the southwest wind
Blows after sunset through the leisuring air,
And on the sky nightly the Charioteer
Leads down the sullen dog-star to his lair,
After the feverous vigil of July,
When the loud pageant of the year's high noon
Passed up the ways of time to sing and part,
Grief also wandered by
From out the lovers and the leaves of June,
And one night at the hiding of the moon
It beckoned me and led me by the heart.
Deep within dreams it led me out of doors
As from the upper vault the night outpours,
And when I saw that to it all the skies
Yearned as a sea asleep yearns to its shores,
It took a little clay and touched my eyes.

And then I saw, then heard —
Multitudes, multitudes, under the moon they stirred!
The weaker brothers of our earthly breed;
Watchmen of whom our safety takes no heed;
Swift helpers of the wind that sowed the seed
Before the first field was or any fruit;
Warriors against the bivouac of the weed;
Earth's earliest ploughmen for the tender root,
All came about my head and at my feet
A thousand, thousand sweet,
With starry eyes not even raised to plead;
Bewildered, driven, hiding, fluttering, mute!

And I beheld and saw them one by one
Pass and become as nothing in the night.
Clothed smooth with red they were who once were white;
Drooping, who once led armies to the sun,
Of whom the lowly grass now topped the flight:
In scarlet faint who once were brave in brown;
Climbers and builders of the silent town,
Creepers and burrowers all in crimson dye,
Winged mysteries of song that from the sky
Once dashed long music down.

O who would take away music from the earth?
Have we so much? Or love upon the hearth?
No more — they faded;
The great trees bending between birth and birth
Sighed for them, and the night wind's hoarse rebuff
Shouted the shame of which I was persuaded.
Shall Nature's only pausing be by men invaded?
Or shall we lay grief's faggots on her shoulders bare?
Has she not borne enough?
Soon will the mirroring woodland pools begin to con her,
And her sad immemorial passion come upon her;
Lo, would you add despair unto despair?
Shall not the Spring be answer to her prayer?
Must her uncomforted heavens overhead,
Weeping, look down on tears and still behold
Only wings broken or a fledgeling dead,
Or underfoot the meadows that wore gold
Die, and the leaves go mourning to the mould
Beneath the dead and desperate feet
Of those who in next summer's meadows shall not meet?

THE LESSER CHILDREN

Who has not seen in the high gulf of light
What, lower, was a bird, but now
Is moored and altered quite
Into an island of unshaded joy?
To whom the mate below upon the bough
Shouts once and brings him from his high employ.
Yet speeding he forgot not of the cloud
Nor of the light he left, burning aloud —
But took a little of the day,
A little of the coloured sky,
And of the joy that would not stay
He wove a song that cannot die.
Then, then — the unfathomable shame;
The one last wrong arose from out the flame,
The ravening hate that hated not was hurled
Bidding the radiant love once more beware,
Bringing one more loneliness on the world,
And one more blindness in the unseen air.

Winds of the fall that all year loud or low
Somewhere upon the earth go wandering,
You saw, you moaned, you know:
Withhold not then unto all time to tell
Lest unborn others of us see this thing.
Bring our sleek, comfortable reason low;
Recount how souls grown tremulous as a bell
Came forth each other and the day to greet
In morning air all Indian Summer-sweet,
And crept upstream, through wood or field or brake,
Most tremblingly to take
What crumbs that from the Master's table fell.
Cry with what thronging thunders they were met,
And hide not how the least leaf was made wet.
Cry till no watcher says that all is well

With raucous discord through the leaning spheres.
But tell
With tears, with tears,
How the last man is harmed even as they
Who on these dawns are fire, at dusk are clay.

What shall be done
By you, shy folk who cease thus heart by heart?
You for whose fate such fate forever hovers?
O little lovers,
If you would still have nests beneath the sun
Gather your broods about you and depart,
Before the stony forward-pressing faces,
Into the lands bereft of any sound,
The solemn and compassionate desert places.
Give unto men no more the strong delight
To know that underneath the frozen ground
Dwells the warm life and all the quick, pure lore.
Take from our eyes the glory of great flight.
Let us behold no more
People untroubled by a Fate's veiled eyes.
Leave us upon an earth of faith forlorn.
No more wild tidings from the sweet far skies
Of love's long utmost heavenward endeavor.
So shall the silence pour on us for ever
The streaming arrows of unutterable scorn.
Nor shall the cry of famine be a shield
The altar of a brutish mood to hide.
Stains, stains upon the lintels of our doors
Wail to be justified.
Shall there be mutterings at the seasons' yield?
Has eye of man seen bared the granary floors?
Are the fields wasted? Spilled the oil and wine?
Is the fat seed under the clod decayed?

THE LESSER CHILDREN

Does ever the fig tree languish or the vine?
Who has beheld the harvest promise fade?
Or any orchard heavy with fruit asway
Withered away?

No, not these things, but grosser things than these
Are the dim parents of a guilt not dim;
Ancestral urges out of old caves blowing,
When Fear watched at our coming and our going
The horror of the chattering face of Whim.
Hates, cruelties new fallen from the trees
To which we clung with impulse sad for love,
Shames we have had all time to rid us of,
Disgraces cold and sorrows long bewept,
Recalled, revived, and kept,
Unmeaning quarrels, blood-compelling lust,
And snarling woes from our old home, the dust.

Yet even of these one saving shape may rise;
Fear may unveil our eyes.
For who may know what curse of blight would fall
Upon a land bare of the sweet shy races
Who day and night keep ward and seneschal
Upon the treasury of the planted spaces?
Then would the locust have his fill,
And the blind worm lay tithe,
The unfed stones rot in the listless mill,
The sound of grinding cease.
No yearning gold would whisper to the scythe,
Hunger at last would prove us of one blood,
The shores of dream be drowned in tides of need,
Horribly would the whole earth be at peace,
The burden of the grasshopper indeed
Weigh down the green corn and the tender bud,

The plague of Egypt fall upon the wheat,
And the shrill nit would batten in the heat.

But you, O poor of deeds and rich of breath,
Whose eyes have made our eyes a hue abhorred,
Red, eager aids of aid-unneeding Death,
Hunters before the Lord,
If lust of blood come on you like a fiery dart
Pluck a young ash tree or a sapling yew
And at the root end fix an iron thorn,
Then, go with rocking laughter of the horn,
Seek out some burly guardian of the hills
And set your urgent thew against his thew.
Then shall the hidden wisdom and the wills
Strive, and bear witness to the trees and clods
How one has dumb lore of the rocks and swales
And one has reason like unto the gods.
Then shall the lagging righteousness ensue,
The powers at last be equal in the scales,
And the man's club and the beast's claw be flails
To winnow the unworthy of the two.
Then on the earth, in the sky and the heavenly court
That broods behind it,
Justice shall be awakened and aware,
Then those who go forth greatly, seeking sport,
Shall doubtless find it,
And all things be fair.

Ridgely Torrence

BIRDS OF SEA AND SHORE

*"Lone white gull with sickle wings
You reap for the heart inscrutable things."*

TO A SEAMEW

The lark knows no such rapture,
  Such joy no nightingale,
As sways the songless measure
Wherein thy wings take pleasure:
Thy love may no man capture,
  Thy pride may no man quail;
The lark knows no such rapture,
  Such joy no nightingale.

. . . .

Our dreams have wings that falter,
  Our hearts bear hopes that die;
For thee no dream could better
A life no fears may fetter,
A pride no care can alter,
  That wots not whence or why
Our dreams have wings that falter,
  Our hearts bear hopes that die.

With joy more fierce and sweeter
  Than joys we deem divine
Their lives, by time untarnished,
Are girt about and garnished,
Who match the wave's full metre
  And drink the wind's wild wine
With joy more fierce and sweeter
  Than joys we deem divine.

Ah, well were I forever,
  Wouldst thou change lives with me,

And take my song's wild honey,
And give me back thy sunny
Wide eyes that weary never,
   And wings that search the sea;
Ah, well were I forever,
    Wouldst thou change lives with me!

Algernon Charles Swinburne

TO A SEA-BIRD

SAUNTERING hither on listless wings,
  Careless vagabond of the sea,
Little thou heedest the surf that sings,
The bar that thunders, the shale that rings, —
  Give me to keep thy company.

Little thou hast, old friend, that's new;
  Storms and wrecks are old things to thee;
Sick am I of these changes too;
Little to care for, little to rue, —
  I on the shore, and thou on the sea.

All of thy wanderings, far and near,
  Bring thee at last to shore and me;
All of my journeyings end them here,
This our tether must be our cheer, —
  I on the shore, and thou on the sea.

Lazily rocking on ocean's breast,
  Something in common, old friend, have we;
Thou on the shingle seekest thy nest,
I to the waters look for rest, —
  I on the shore, and thou on the sea.

Francis Bret Harte

SANCTUARY

I was on the ocean once
  Nearing the Azores,
It was night and wind was blowing
  Heavy from the shores,

When a flock of tiny land birds,
  Swept too far to sea,
Came within the lighted vessel
  For security.

Every beam and gilded cornice
  Black with tired wings, —
Such a refuge in wild ocean
  Only fancy brings.

There they slept till daylight called them
  To the air again,
Crying to us as they vanished,
  "All the world is kin!"

Elinor MacArthur

THE LITTLE BEACH-BIRD

Thou little bird, thou dweller by the sea,
  Why takest thou its melancholy voice,
    And with that boding cry
    Why o'er the waves dost fly?
O, rather, bird, with me
  Through the fair land rejoice!

Thy flitting form comes ghostly dim and pale
  As driven by a beating storm at sea;

Thy cry is weak and scared,
  As if thy mates had shared
The doom of us. Thy wail, —
  What doth it bring to me?

Thou callest along the sand, and hauntest the surge,
  Restless, and sad; as if, in strange accord
    With the motion and the roar
    Of waves that drive to shore,
One spirit did ye urge —
  The Mystery — the Word.

Of thousands, thou, both sepulchre and pall,
  Old Ocean! A requiem o'er the dead,
    From out thy gloomy cells,
    A tale of mourning tells, —
Tells of man's woe and fall,
  His sinless glory fled.

Then turn thee, little bird, and take thy flight
  Where the complaining sea shall sadness bring
    Thy spirit nevermore.
    Come, quit with me the shore,
For gladness and the light,
  Where birds of summer sing.

Richard Henry Dana

THE SANDPIPER

Across the narrow beach we flit,
  One little sandpiper and I,
And fast I gather, bit by bit,
  The scattered driftwood bleached and dry.

THE SANDPIPER

The wild waves reach their hands for it,
    The wild wind raves, the tide runs high,
As up and down the beach we flit, —
    One little sandpiper and I.

Above our heads the sullen clouds
    Scud black and swift across the sky;
Like silent ghosts in misty shrouds
    Stand out the white lighthouses high.
Almost as far as eye can reach
    I see the close-reefed vessels fly,
As fast we flit along the beach, —
    One little sandpiper and I.

I watch him as he skims along,
    Uttering his sweet and mournful cry.
He starts not at my fitful song,
    Or flash of fluttering drapery.
He has no thought of any wrong;
    He scans me with a fearless eye:
Staunch friends are we, well tried and strong,
    The little sandpiper and I.

Comrade, where wilt thou be to-night
    When the loosed storm breaks furiously?
My driftwood fire will burn so bright!
    To what warm shelter canst thou fly?
I do not fear for thee, though wroth
    The tempest rushes through the sky:
For are we not God's children both,
    Thou, little sandpiper, and I?

Celia Thaxter

THE SANDPIPER

Along the sea-edge, like a gnome
Or rolling pebble in the foam,
As though he timed the ocean's throbbing,
Runs a piper, bobbing, bobbing.

Now he stiffens, now he wilts,
Like a little boy on stilts!
Creatures burrow, insects hide,
When they see the piper glide.

You would think him out of joint,
Till his bill began to point.
You would doubt if he could fly,
Till his straightness arrows by.

You would take him for a clown,
Till he peeps and flutters down,
Vigilant among the grasses,
Where a fledgling bobs and passes.

Witter Bynner

THE SANDPIPER

Prime indignity of solitude —
To smile! But smiles intrude
When thou, so tipsy biped,
Teetering on twine-legs and toes of thread
Through the thin surf-lace,
Cry thy very name and place
In uncompanioned fear — alarmed
Of man, of me, unarmed

THE SANDPIPER

With any weapon worse
Than irony or any curse
But Titan-laughter. Even thy grace
Would scarce invite my greed,
So much as win my sympathy —
As one with thee!
Scant wonder that thy hammer-head
Cannot look up — with such a bodkin tail
And crop of indescribable wet feed!
Silence would avail
More than thy frantic piping, much —
With that quaint running-gear and such
An insufficient wing to clutch
The air that lends the sea-gull speed.
Scarcely risen from your tracks before
You falter and dip down,
Like a vellum toy
Cast on the wind by a coolie boy,
Or like some wing-trousered clown
Ascending gloriously to the floor
Whence he but started —
And returned ere he departed.

But the Maker, fashioning the eagle,
Fashioned thee, dear little wader,
To the perfect pattern of His hand!
Perfect in thy way, as regal
As a king-seal, and man's persuader
Of his own futility in slipping sand!
The Carpenter of thy splint frame
And that unreasoning child-cry
Matched thy tenderness in every poet's eye —
To guard thy innocence and praise thy name.

Ivan Swift

SEA-STRETCH

(The Pelicans)

A GOLDEN day
Fringed with grey shadows
Of the dunes.
Shore-grass that shines as lances
In the sun:
Flapping silhouettes of pelicans
Drift by
On out to sea,
Sketched against the canvas
Of the heaven
By the Master of Design.

Surf-roar and shining of the sun,
Sand-drift and wind-drift, —
All are forgotten
As the spreading wings above
Rise higher toward the canyons
Where the clouds patrol the day.
What seek they —
The old, eternal quiet
Of the King's Highway?
While you and I sit idly by
And wonder as we may.

The shadows of the sand-dunes
Lie grey along the shore:
The shadows of the pelicans
Drift where the breakers roar.
Far, far above the sea-stretch
And the lance-grass salt with spray,
The pelicans are flying
Against the golden day!

Rena Sheffield

TO A SEA-GULL

Bird of the fierce delight,
Brother of foam as white
And winged as foam is,
Wheeling again from flight
To some unfooted height
Where your blithe home is;

Bird of the wind and spray,
Crying by night and day
Sorrowful laughter,
How shall man's thought survey
Your will or your wings' way,
Or follow after?

What pride is man's, and why,
Angel of air, should I
Joy to be human?
You walk and swim and fly,
Laugh like a man and cry
Like any woman.

I would your spirit were mine
When your wings dip and shine,
Smoothly advancing:
I drink a breathless wine
Of speed in your divine
Aerial dancing.

Arthur Symons

SEA-GULL

Sea-gull swooping,
   Swerving, wheeling,
You that live
   With the sky for ceiling,
You know the feel of being free!
   Give it to me!

You know the feel of spurning the ground!
See, I am bound.
I have a thousand bonds to hold
My feet to the ground. You fly and are bold!
I have duties and rules for chain.
You fly free in the fog and rain
And the mist and storm! Up into the sun.
You fly;
And are one
With the sky!
But I ——

You have the gift of being free.
Give it, just for an hour, to me!
                Mary Carolyn Davies

THE ONSET

The wet sands were grey-blue that afternoon
   We stood on the wide dune,
And watched the gleeful waves come racing far
   And farther up the bar
Until, to each new vantage of the race,
   We must give place.

The gulls, a multitude upon the sand,
   Seeking the friendly succor of the land,
Retreated at each onset of the wave,
   Then moved back, imperturbable and grave,
Till, in a swift accord, they took the sky
   With strident cry.

We, on that void immensity of beach,
   Turned with our human longing each to each,
Knowing how brief the years that one may cheat
   The mounting wave of time that seeks his feet.
Yet, like the sea-bird winging tempest high,
   Love can defy.

Jessie B. Rittenhouse

TO A SOLITARY SEA-GULL

Lone white gull with sickle wings,
You reap for the heart inscrutable things:
Sorrow of mists and surf of the shore,
Winds that sigh of the nevermore;
Fret of foam and flurry of rain,
Swept far over the troubled tide;
Maths of mystery and grey pain
The sea's voice ever yields, beside.
Lone white gull, you reap for the heart
Life's most sad and inscrutable part.

Cale Young Rice

SEA-BIRDS

O lonesome sea-gull, floating far
   Over the ocean's icy waste,

Aimless and wide thy wanderings are,
　　Forever vainly seeking rest: —
　　Where is thy mate, and where thy nest?

'Twixt wintry sea and wintry sky,
　　Cleaving the keen air with thy breast,
Thou sailest slowly, solemnly;
　　No fetter on thy wing is pressed: —
　　Where is thy mate, and where thy nest?

O restless, homeless human soul,
　　Following for aye thy nameless quest,
The gulls float, and the billows roll;
　　Thou watchest still, and questionest; —
　　Where is thy mate, and where thy nest?
Elizabeth Akers Allen

SEA-BIRDS

Birds that float upon a wave,
　　Resting from the tiring air,
Be the hopes that I would save
　　From despair.

Menaced by the sky above,
　　Menaced by the deep below,
You rock as on the breast of love
　　To and fro.

If immensities like these
　　Cannot fright a thing so frail,
I will keep my heart at ease
　　In the gale.
Elinor MacArthur

GULLS OVER GREAT SALT LAKE

WHAT do they here, these denizens of the deep,
These wingèd hosts
Round the inhospitable coasts
Of this vast inland mere?
Their kin I saw but late
About the Golden Gate.
Beauty was there —
Charm everywhere;
Here all is bleak, gaunt, bare,
A desolation so immense
That it impales the sense;
No living thing
Save the gray gulls a-wing.

They seem exiled
In this vast wild,
This wilderness of arid height and shore;
No spindrift-crested wave
Surges for them to brave;
Do they not crave
The ocean's multitudinous charge and roar?
I hear their cries
Go up against the brazen arch of skies;
Are they the cries of longing? Who shall say?
Somehow I hold them alien to this place,
Linking them with the sea,
Beneath the windy span of night and day,
Its rapt immensity,
Its mighty space.

Whether or no they yearn
I may not learn.

I leave them here, the one fair memory
Of beauty and of grace
In all this drear,
Remote and brooding mountain-girdled mere.

Ross Sutphen

THE STORMY PETREL

A THOUSAND miles from land are we,
Tossing about on the roaring sea, —
From billow to bounding billow cast,
Like fleecy snow on the stormy blast.
The sails are scattered abroad like weeds;
The strong masts shake like quivering reeds;
The mighty cables and iron chains,
The hull, which all earthly strength disdains, —
They strain and they creak; and hearts like stone
Their natural hard, proud strength disown.

Up and down! — up and down!
From the base of the wave to the billow's crown,
And amidst the flashing and feathery foam
The stormy petrel finds a home, —
A home, if such a place may be
For her who lives on the wide, wide sea,
On the craggy ice, in the frozen air,
And only seeketh her rocky lair
To warm her young, and to teach them to spring
At once o'er the waves on their stormy wing!

O'er the deep! — o'er the deep!
Where the whale and the shark and the swordfish
    sleep, —

Outflying the blast and the driving rain,
The petrel telleth her tale — in vain;
For the mariner curseth the warning bird
Which bringeth him news of the storm unheard!
Ah, thus does the prophet of good or ill
Meet hate from the creatures he serveth still;
Yet he ne'er falters, — so, petrel, spring
Once more o'er the waves on thy stormy wing!
Bryan Waller Procter

TO A PETREL

ALL day long in the spindrift swinging,
Bird of the sea! bird of the sea!
How I would that I had thy winging —
How I envy thee!

How I would that I had thy spirit,
So to careen, joyous to cry,
Over the storm and never fear it!
Into the night that hovers near it,
Calm on a reeling sky!

All day long, and the night, unresting!
Ah, I believe thy every breath
Means that life's best comes ever breasting
Peril and pain and death!
Cale Young Rice

TO THE MAN-OF-WAR-BIRD

THOU who hast slept all night upon the storm
Waking renewed on thy prodigious pinions,

(Burst the wild storm? above it thou ascended'st,
And rested on the sky, thy slave that cradled thee,)
Now a blue point, far, far in heaven floating,
As to the light emerging here on deck I watch thee,
(Myself a speck, a point on the world's floating vast.)

Far, far at sea,
After the night's fierce drifts have strewn the shore
    with wrecks,
With re-appearing day as now so happy and serene,
The rosy and elastic dawn, the flashing sun,
The limpid spread of air cerulean,
Thou also re-appearest.

Thou born to match the gale, (thou art all wings,)
To cope with heaven and earth and sea and hurricane,
Thou ship of air that never furl'st thy sails,
Days, even weeks untired and onward, through
    spaces, realms gyrating,
At dusk that look'st on Senegal, at morn America,
That sport'st amid the lightning-flash and thunder-
    cloud,
In them, in thy experiences, hadst thou my soul,
What joys! what joys were thine!

Walt Whitman

ALBATROSS

TIME cannot age thy sinews, nor the gale
Batter the network of thy feathered mail,
  Lone sentry of the deep!
Among the crashing caverns of the storm,
With wing unfettered, lo! thy frigid form
  Is whirled in dreamless sleep!

ALBATROSS

Where shall thy wing find rest for all its might?
Where shall thy lidless eye, that scours the night,
   Grow blank in utter death?
When shall thy thousand years have stripped thee
        bare,
Invulnerable spirit of the air,
   And sealed thy giant breath?

Not till thy bosom hugs the icy wave, —
Not till thy palsied limbs sink in that grave,
   Caught by the shrieking blast,
And hurled upon the sea with broad wings locked,
On an eternity of waters rocked,
   Defiant to the last!

Charles Warren Stoddard

BIRDS OF LAKE AND RIVER, MARSH AND MOOR

*"I heard the wild geese flying
In the dead of night."*

"Lone swan whose troubled cry the midnight hears."

THE HERON

O MELANCHOLY bird, a winter's day
Thou standest by the margin of the pool,
And, taught by God, dost thy whole being school
By patience, which all evil can allay.
God has appointed thee the fish thy prey;
And given thee a lesson to the fool
Unthrifty, to submit to moral rule,
And his unthinking course by thee to weigh.
There need not schools nor the professor's chair,
Though these be good, true wisdom to impart;
He, who has not enough for these to spare
Of time, or gold, may yet amend his heart,
And teach his soul, by brooks and rivers fair:
Nature is always wise in every part.
            Edward Hovell-Thurlow

DAWN IN THE EVERGLADES

ONE day, while still the dawn denied the call
Of sentient life, which waits upon her whim,
I watched the marshes gray with fog and all
A-drip with dew which framed each sedgy rim;

And there, beyond a line of mist, there rose
A bank of trees, their branches studded white
With living flowers which seemed to sleep or doze,
Awaiting flight's impulsion with the light.

A moment's hush — then up from out the east
Slim fingers of auroral tintings broke

And filled the world. The tender glow increased.
It touched the ghostly flowers; they stirred, awoke —

A cloud of snowy herons, darkness done,
Flew east, along the air-ways to the sun.
                              Halle W. Warlow

THE BLUE HERON

Where water-grass grows overgreen
   On damp cool flats by gentle streams,
Still as a ghost and sad of mien,
   With half-closed eyes the heron dreams.

Above him in the sycamore
   The flicker beats a dull tattoo;
Through papaw groves the soft airs pour
   Gold dust of blooms and fragrance new.

And from the thorn it loves so well,
   The oriole flings out its strong,
Sharp lay, wrought in the crucible
   Of its flame-circled soul of song.

The heron nods. The charming runes
   Of Nature's music thrill his dreams;
The joys of many Mays and Junes
   Wash past him like cool summer streams.

What tranquil life, what joyful rest,
   To feel the touch of fragrant grass,
And doze like him, while tenderest
   Dream-waves across my sleep should pass!
                              Maurice Thompson

THE HERONS ON BO ISLAND

The herons on Bo Island
   Stand solemnly all day;
Like lean old men together
   They hump their shoulders grey.
Oh, I wish I could get near them
   To hear the things they say!

They turn up their coat collars
   And stand so gloomily;
And somehow, as I watch them,
   It always seems to me
That in their trouser pockets
   Their wrinkled hands must be.

But if I venture near them
   They look at me in doubt,
And with great wings loose-flapping
   They circle round about,
Their long legs hanging downwards,
   Their slim necks all stretched out.

If I stood on Bo Island
   As gloomily as they,
And ruffled up my collar
   And hid my hands away,
It might be they would join me
   And I'd hear the things they say.

Elizabeth Shane

THE VILLAGE STORK

The old Hercynian Forest sent
   His weather on the plain;
Wahlwinkel's orchards writhed and bent
   In whirls of wind and rain.
Within her nest, upon the roof,
For generations tempest-proof,
Wahlwinkel's stork with her young ones lay,
When the hand of the hurricane tore away
   The house and the home that held them.

The storm passed by; the happy trees
   Stood up and kissed the sun;
And from the birds new melodies
   Came fluting one by one.
The stork, upon the paths below,
Went sadly pacing to and fro,
With dripping plumes and head depressed,
For she thought of the spoiled ancestral nest,
   And the old, inherited honor.

"Behold her now!" the throstle sang
   From out the linden tree;
"Who knows from what a line she sprang,
   Beyond the unknown sea?"
"If she could sing, perchance her tale
Might move us," chirruped the nightingale.
"Sing? She can only rattle and creak!"
Whistled the bullfinch, with silver beak,
   Within the wires of his prison.

And all the birds there, or loud or low,
   Were one in scoff and scorn;

THE VILLAGE STORK

But still the stork paced to and fro,
   As utterly forlorn.
Then suddenly, in turn of eye,
   She saw a poet passing by,
And the thought in his brain was an arrow of fire,
That pierced her with passion and pride and ire,
   And gave her a voice to answer.

She raised her head and shook her wings,
   And faced the piping crowd.
"Best service," said she, "never sings.
   True honor is not loud.
My kindred carol not, nor boast;
Yet we are loved and welcomed most,
And our ancient race is dearest and first,
And the hand that hurts us is held accursed
   In every home of Wahlwinkel!

"Beneath a sky forever fair,
   And with a summer sod,
The land I come from smiles — and there
   My brother was a god!
My nest upon a temple stands
And sees the shine of desert lands;
And the palm and the tamarisk cool my wings,
When the blazing beam of the noonday stings,
   And I drink from the holy river!

"There I am sacred, even as here;
   Yet dare I not be lost,
When meads are bright, hearts full of cheer,
   At blithesome Pentecost.
Then from mine obelisk I depart,
Guided by something in my heart,

And sweep in a line over Libyan sands
To the blossoming olives by Grecian lands,
  And rest on the Cretan Ida!

"Parnassus sees me as I sail;
  I cross the Adrian brine;
The distant summits fade and fail,
  Dalmatian, Apennine;
The Alpine snows beneath me gleam,
I see the yellow Danube stream;
But I hasten on till my spent wings fall
Where I bring a blessing to each and all,
  And babes to the wives of Wahlwinkel!"

She drooped her head and spake no more;
  The birds on either hand
Sang louder, lustier than before —
  They could not understand.
Thus mused the stork, with snap of beak;
"Better be silent than to speak!
Highest being can never be taught:
They have their voices, I my thought;
  And they were never in Egypt!"

Bayard Taylor

THE HERALD CRANE

Ah! say you so, bold sailor
  In the sun-lit depths of sky?
Dost thou so soon the seed-time tell
  In thy imperial cry,
As circling in yon shoreless sea
  Thine unseen form goes drifting by?

THE HERALD CRANE

I can not trace in the noon-day glare
   Thy regal flight, O crane!
From the leaping might of the fiery light
   Mine eyes recoil in pain,
But on mine ear thine echoing cry
   Falls like a bugle strain.

The mellow soil glows beneath my feet,
   Where lies the buried grain;
The warm light floods the length and breadth
   Of the vast, dim, shimmering plain,
Throbbing with heat and the nameless thrill
   Of the birth-time's restless pain.

On weary wing, plebeian geese
   Push on their arrowy line
Straight into the north, or snowy brant
   In dazzling sunshine, gloom and shine;
But thou, O crane, save for thy sovereign cry,
   At thy majestic height
On proud, extended wings sweep'st on
   In lonely, easeful flight.

Then cry, thou martial-throated herald!
   Cry to the sun, and sweep
And swing along thy mateless, tireless course
   Above the clouds that sleep
Afloat on lazy air — cry on! Send down
   Thy trumpet note — it seems
The voice of hope and dauntless will,
   And breaks the spell of dreams.

                      Hamlin Garland

WITH THE MALLARD DRAKE

Oh, for a day in the white wind's cheek!
   To share the mallard's stroke of power,
The electric spark in the tip of his beak,
   And flying a hundred miles an hour!
With his throbbing pulse the air to beat —
   The swift wild duck, the beautiful thing!
The strength of the sun in his yellow feet,
     The purple of night asleep on his breast,
     The green of a thousand Junes on his crest,
   The bank of the heavens across his wing!

To alight and drink in the frothing rings
   That circle away to the greening gap;
To stop for the noonday feast of kings —
   The crimson seeds in the marsh's lap;
To forget where the city's white flags burn,
   And know but the deep air's quivering thrills;
The mystery of his flight to learn,
     To follow the way the wild duck takes,
     To the twilight of the grassy lakes,
   To the glory of the Yukon hills.

To rest where the old gray sea-towers shake;
   'Mong tangled moss and grassy knots
To seek the haunt of the kittiwake
   And the pointed eggs with blood-red spots.
O kittiwake of the snow-white crown,
   Of the coral feet and vermilion-eyed,
Of the tender croon and wings of down,
     I would fly with you this burning day
     To the wind-swept peaks away, away,
   And hide where you and the tempest hide.

Oh, for a day in the waltzing wind,
   With the mallard in his swift strong flight!
To leave the blue frost-smoke behind,
   And poise in the Yukon's opal light;
To know the rush of the upper airs,
   The curve of the wing-tip thrilling through
The swelling soul of him who dares!
     O beautiful bird, bronze night on thy breast,
     A thousand golden Junes in thy crest,
   And across thy wing heaven's bar of blue!

Anonymous

TO A WILD GOOSE OVER DECOYS

O LONELY trumpeter, coasting down the sky,
Like a winter leaf blown from a bur-oak tree
By whipping winds, and flapping silverly
Against the sun — I know your lonely cry.

I know the worn wild heart that bends your flight
And circles you above this beckoning lake,
Eager of neck, to find the honking drake
Who speaks of reedy refuge through the night.

I know the sudden rapture that you fling
In answer to our friendly gander's call —
Halloo! Beware decoys! — or you will fall
With a silver bullet whistling in your wing!

Beat on your weary flight across the blue!
Beware, O traveler, of our gabbling geese!
Beware this weedy counterfeit of peace! —
Oh, I was once a passing bird like you.

Lew Sarett

ETCHING AT DUSK

I HAVE just seen three ducks rise up from the rushes
And swing into the evening, into the night,
Over the water, over the rushes beyond it,
Not too swiftly, there still lies a sword of light
Yonder between the cattails and the willows.
It will be gone soon; soon this splendid drake
Too will have gone. Even now he is lost in the twilight,
Calling and calling and calling over the lake.

Frederic Prokosch

THE WILD DUCK

A STRANGE thing, that a lark and robin sky
Should drop a wild duck on a little pond
Where cattle drink! — Strange that a duck should fly
Down here, when there are lakes a day beyond!
Slowly it drags across the silken green
Two silver threads — and fastens them quite near,
As if the seam were done. Perhaps the sheen,
Reflecting an old moonlight, drew it here.
Strange that your eye should waver on the sight
When it has guided death so oft before
To innocence as wild!... And stranger still,
A wild duck should withhold its wings from flight,
As if it had no heart for flying more,
And calmly waited, knowing you would kill.

Leroy McLeod

WILD GEESE

How oft against the sunset sky or moon
    I watched that moving zigzag of spread wings

In unforgotten autumns gone too soon,
  In unforgotten springs.

Creatures of desolation, far they fly
  Above all lands bound by the curling foam;
In misty fens, wild moors and trackless sky
  These wild things have their home.

They know the tundra of Siberian coasts,
  And tropic marshes by the Indian seas;
They know the clouds and night and starry hosts
  From Crux to Pleiades.

Dark flying rune against the western glow —
  It tells the sweep and loneliness of things,
Symbol of autumns vanished long ago,
  Symbol of coming springs!

Frederick Peterson

TO A WATERFOWL

Whither, midst falling dew,
While glow the heavens with the last steps of day,
Far, through their rosy depths, dost thou pursue
  Thy solitary way?

  Vainly the fowler's eye
Might mark thy distant flight to do thee wrong,
As, darkly painted on the crimson sky,
  Thy figure floats along.

  Seek'st thou the plashy brink
Of weedy lake, or marge of river wide,

Or where the rocking billows rise and sink
   On the chafed ocean-side?

There is a Power whose care
Teaches thy way along that pathless coast, —
The desert and illimitable air, —
   Lone wandering, but not lost.

All day thy wings have fanned
At that far height, the cold, thin atmosphere,
Yet stoop not, weary, to the welcome land,
   Though the dark night is near.

And soon that toil shall end;
Soon shalt thou find a summer home, and rest,
And scream among thy fellows; reeds shall bend,
   Soon, o'er thy sheltered nest.

Thou'rt gone, the abyss of heaven
Hath swallowed up thy form; yet, on my heart
Deeply hath sunk the lesson thou hast given,
   And shall not soon depart.

He who, from zone to zone,
Guides through the boundless sky thy certain flight,
In the long way that I must tread alone,
   Will lead my steps aright.

William Cullen Bryant

THE FLIGHT OF THE GEESE

I HEAR the low wind wash the softening snow,
   The low tide loiter down the shore. The night,
   Full filled with April forecast, hath no light.
The salt wave on the sedge-flat pulses slow.

Through the hid furrows lisp in murmurous flow
   The thaw's shy ministers; and hark! the height
   Of heaven grows weird and loud with unseen flight
Of strong hosts prophesying as they go!

High through the drenched and hollow night their wings
   Beat northward hard on winter's trail. The sound
     Of their confused and solemn voices, borne
     Athwart the dark to their long Arctic morn,
   Comes with a sanction and an awe profound,
A boding of unknown, foreshadowed things.
Charles G. D. Roberts

THE WILD GEESE COME OVER NO MORE

The wild geese come over no more
As when I was a boy
With their high sweet honking
That lifts the heart with joy.

Their chill aery paths are changed,
The lake awaits in vain
For a tired wing to drop to it
And rise at dawn again.

The wild thoughts of my high youth
Have left my heart too —
Driven away by the hard huntsmen,
Memory, care, and rue.
Cale Young Rice

WILD GEESE

I HEARD the wild geese flying
　In the dead of night,
With beat of wings and crying
I heard the wild geese flying.
And dreams in my heart sighing
　Followed their northward flight.
I heard the wild geese flying
　In the dead of night.

Eleanor Chipp

WILD GEESE

I HOLD to my heart when the geese are flying —
A wavering wedge on the high bright blue —
I tighten my lips to keep from crying
"Beautiful birds — let me go with you!"

And at night when they honk — and their wings are
　　　weaving
A pattern across a full gold moon —
I hold to a heart that would be leaving
If it were freed to fly too soon.

I hold to a heart that would be going
A comrade to wild birds of the air —
As wayward as they — and never knowing
Where it is going — and never care.

I hold to my heart — for here lies duty,
And here is the path where my feet must stray —
But O that quivering line of beauty
Beating its beautiful, bright-winged way!

Grace Noll Crowell

GRAY GEESE FLYING

Gray geese over the rock-ribbed hill, solemnly
Flying, solemnly making your certain way:
There are souls I have known like you, unstirred,
 untrembling,
Moving like you, O gray

Wild geese, who may not ever wander alone
On perilous journeys, but must go a-flying
Desperately straight, in a parade, together,
Crying, crying.

Frederic Prokosch

THE LOON

A lonely lake, a lonely shore,
A lone pine leaning on the moon;
All night the water-beating wings
Of a solitary loon.

With mournful wail from dusk to dawn
He gibbered at the taunting stars —
A hermit-soul gone raving mad.
And beating at his bars.

Lew Sarett

THE LOON

Tameless in his stately pride, along the lake of islands,
  Tireless speeds the lonely loon upon his diving
   track; —
Emerald and gold emblazon, satin-like, his shoulder,
  Ebony and pearl inlay, mosaic-like, his back.

THE LOON

Sailing, thus sailing, thus sails the brindled loon,
When the wave rolls black with storm, or sleeps in summer noon.

Sailing through the islands, oft he lifts his loud bravura; —
  Clarion-clear it rings, and round ethereal trumpets swell; —
Upward looks the feeding deer, he sees the aiming hunter,
  Up and then away, the loon has warned his comrade well.
Sailing, thus sailing, thus sails the brindled loon,
Pealing on the solitude his sounding bugle-tune.

Long before the eagle furls his pinion on the pine-top,
  Long before the bluebird gleams in sapphire through the glen,
Long before the lily blots the shoal with golden apples,
  Leaves the loon his southern sun to sail the lake again.
Sailing, then sailing, then sails the brindled loon,
Leading with his shouting call the Spring's awakening croon.

Long after bitter chills have pierced the windy water,
  Long after Autumn dies all dolphin-like away;
Long after coat of russet dons the deer for winter,
  Plies the solitary loon his cold and curdled bay.
Sailing, there sailing, there sails the brindled loon,
Till in chains no more to him the lake yields watery boon.

Alfred Billings Street

THE WATER OUZEL

Little brown surf-bather of the mountains!
Spirit of foam, lover of cataracts, shaking your wings
 in falling waters!
Have you no fear of the roar and rush when Nevada
 plunges —
Nevada, the shapely dancer, feeling her way with slim
 white fingers?
How dare you dash at Yosemite the mighty —
Tall, white-limbed Yosemite, leaping down, down over
 the cliff?
Is it not enough to lean on the blue of mountains?
Is it not enough to rest with your mate at timberline,
 in bushes that hug the rocks?
Must you fly through mad waters where the heaped-up
 granite breaks them?
Must you batter your wings in the torrent?
Must you plunge for life and death through the foam?
Harriet Monroe

TO AN UPLAND PLOVER

Crescent-winged, sky-clean
 Hermit of pastures wild,
  Upland plover, shy-souled lover
 Of field ways undefiled!
I watch your curve-tipt pinion gleam —
Slim as a scythe — the rusty green
  Reaches of sweet-fern cover
That slant to your secret glade,
But what you cull with your rhythmic blade
  What mortal can discover?

Azure-born, gale-blown
  Gull of the billowy hills!
    My heart goes forth to see you hover
  So far from human sills,
To hear your tweeting, shrill and lone,
Make from the moorgrass such sharp moan
    As some unshriven lover,
For you are sorrow-wise
With memory, whose passions rise
    Whence no man may discover.

Reticent, rare of song,
  Rears the shy soul its pain:
    You sought no cottage eave as cover
  To dole a dulcet plain;
But swift on pinions lithe and strong,
You sought a place for your wild wrong
    God only might discover,
And there God, calling, came,
And flies with you in His white flame —
    Your wilding mate, O plover!

Percy MacKaye

THERE ARE STILL KINGFISHERS

FAITH, peace and joy to-day brings; all has failed
I this day put my hand to, well know I;
Less blind than some so far, though that's not why;
But with joy, peace and faith my spirit is mailed,
Since on Wren's bridge at noon, unseen, unhailed,
I, all alone, saw the kingfisher fly.

Not as before, startled by friendly prod,
In stagnant ditch to imagine something quiver,

Lost while half-seen; but brilliant, clear, and broad,
Forty-two yards up the middle of the river
Under my eyes shot the turquoise unflawed!
Nothing of me that bird knows and will never;
But I rejoiced, as men rejoice in God,
Not that He cares for them, but lives forever.
A. Y. Campbell

THE KINGFISHER [1]

It was the Rainbow gave thee birth,
   And left thee all her lovely hues;
And, as her mother's name was Tears,
   So runs it in thy blood to choose
For haunts the lonely pools, and keep
In company with trees that weep.

Go you and, with such glorious hues,
   Live with proud peacocks in green parks;
On lawns as smooth as shining glass,
   Let every feather show its marks;
Get thee on boughs and clap thy wings
Before the windows of proud kings.

Nay, lovely bird, thou art not vain;
   Thou hast no proud ambitious mind:
I also love a quiet place
   That's green, away from all mankind;
A lonely pool, and let a tree
Sigh with her bosom over me.

William H. Davies

[1] The English kingfisher differs in plumage from the American.

THE SWAN

Hawks stir the blood like fiercely ringing bells
Or far-off bugles;
Even on their perches
They are all latent fury and sheathed power;
And peacocks trail the glory of the world.
But calm, white calm, was born into a swan
To float forever upon moon-smoothed waters
Cool placid breast against cool mirrored breast
And wings curved like great petals
And long throat
Bent dreamily
To listen to the ripple
That widens slowly in a tranquil arrow
Reaching the shores, and lisping on the sand.

Elizabeth Coatsworth

SWANS

With wings held close and slim neck bent,
Along dark water scarcely stirred,
Floats, glimmering and indolent,
The alabaster bird.

Its mate floats near, the lovely one;
They lie like snow, cool flake on flake,
Mild breast on breast of dimmer swan
Dim-mirrored in the lake.

They glide... and glides that white embrace,
Shy bird to bird, with never a sound;
Thus leaned Narcissus toward his face,
Leaned lower till he drowned.

Leda leaned thus, subdued and spent
Beneath those vivid wings of love;
Along the lake, proud, indolent,
The vast birds scarcely move.

Silence is wisdom. Then how wise
Are these whose song is but their knell!
A god did well to choose this guise.
Truly a god did well.

Leonora Speyer

LONE SWAN

DELAY your flight, delay your swift pursuit,
  Lone swan whose troubled cry the midnight hears,
Vibrant along the high aerial route
  Shaking my spirit even unto tears;
I sense the urge that drives you, far behind,
  To join the flock you veered from, gone astray,
Your desperate endeavoring to find
  The guide you lost along a perilous way.

O wind-tossed, weary, now delay your quest!
  Since over-striving is of doubtful worth;
From struggling heights sink quietly to rest
  With straining pinions folded to the earth,
Beside still waters brooding, till you gain
New strength to climb your altitudes of pain.

Rose Mills Powers

THE WILD SWANS AT COOLE

THE trees are in their autumn beauty,
The woodland paths are dry,

THE WILD SWANS AT COOLE

Under the October twilight the water
Mirrors a still sky;
Upon the brimming water among the stones
Are nine and fifty swans.

The nineteenth Autumn has come upon me
Since I first made my count;
I saw, before I had well finished,
All suddenly mount
And scatter wheeling in great broken rings
Upon their clamorous wings.

I have looked upon those brilliant creatures,
And now my heart is sore.
All's changed since I, hearing at twilight,
The first time on this shore,
The bell-beat of their wings above my head
Trod with a lighter tread.

Unwearied still, lover by lover,
They paddle in the cold
Companionable streams or climb the air;
Their hearts have not grown old;
Passion or conquest, wander where they will,
Attend upon them still.

But now they drift on the still water
Mysterious, beautiful;
Among what rushes will they build,
By what lake's edge or pool
Delight men's eyes, when I awake some day
To find they have flown away?

William Butler Yeats

BIRDS OF THE NIGHT

*"And the lone wood-bird — Hark,
The whip-poor-will night long
Threshing the summer dark
With his dim flail of song!"*

A BIRD SINGS AT NIGHT

Who sings upon the pinnacle of night?
   Down, down, unearthly bird, you sing too soon!
O bird, be still! O bird, the earth is stricken
   To hear you at the bosom of the moon.

Consent to silence and a simple dark;
   Permit the heart to lie within the breast
Unveiled before a thousand memories,
   And in parade salute the loveliest.

Permit the heart, unaltered by your singing,
   To have within the dark its pensive way.
Release the heart amid its joys and sorrows
   Untroubled by what angels have to say.

Unhindered comes the dawn, and you may sing
   Victorious and vocal to the light.
But now delay, and let the heart reverse
   Time's sinister profile on the wall of night.
Hildegarde Flanner

ON HEARING A BIRD SING AT NIGHT

Out of what ancient summer of soft airs
   Was spun this song that stills each listening leaf —
This silver, moon-bright minstreling that fares
   Through all old time, still laden with a grief?
Some hidden bird, by turrets and black bars,
   Where one had languished for her face was fair,
Heard thus some troubadour beneath the stars,
   And learned this song of vanished hands and hair.

Who knows what golden story first gave birth
   To this old music that is heavy-sweet
With gardens long forgotten of the earth,
   With passion that was silver wings and feet,
To cross the silent centuries and be heard,
Calling again in this dream-troubled bird!
David Morton

A SOUTHERN WHIP-POOR-WILL

Last night it was the whip-poor-will
Amid the palm-trees by the lake,
With its old piercing, poignant thrill
That banished sleep and bade us wake;
As underneath some northern hill
Last night it was the whip-poor-will.

Spirit or bird, what do you here
Mid the palmettos and the palms,
Flinging your voice so cool and clear
Across the southern midnight calms?
You are a memory that plays
About the dusk of other days:

A memory sweet as jasmine is;
On wings of dream you waft us where
The hills uplift like harmonies
Athwart the blue ethereal air,
And there you sing, ecstatic still,
Enthralling us, O whip-poor-will!
Clinton Scollard

WHIP-POOR-WILL

The whip-poor-will, through the crystal starlight,
Stabbed my memory
With his three-pronged fork of song.

He roused me to forsaken homage
Of old apple trees, just now
In the dream of budding.

He tossed me fancies
Of an old stone wall, where currants
Grow into baby greenness.

And then he pierced me
With his solemn echoes
From my distant woodland.

Philip Cummings

THE WHIP-POOR-WILL

When early summer called us back
    To river, weir and hill,
We two would take the old-time track
    To hear the whip-poor-will.

Twilight would find us, you and I,
    Along the river way,
Intent to hear his far lone cry
    Until the shut of day.

It chanced that we were gone a year,
    And in June's longest light
We waited down beside the weir
    The soft, delaying night.

But all the air was void of song,
   Though we stood rapt and still
And waited for his passion long —
   There was no whip-poor-will.

"It is the Voice Unheard," you said,
   "The hope that may not be" —
When on the instant overhead
   There pierced his litany.

It falls, Belovèd, you are ill
   And take the walk no more,
But now at night he sings at will
   In the plum tree by our door.
Anonymous

NIGHT–HAWK

The night-hawk goes up to the light
Lingering over coming night.

His slender wings have mirrors under
Their slow sweep of peace and wonder,

Twin heliographs to relay on
Brave words of the sun that's gone.

There is not among the birds
A grace so out of reach of words.

So thin and beautiful a scroll
Against the sky that day seems whole;

After things at six and seven
Here is calligraphy of heaven.

Up. Then like a falling star
He falls with a brief, celestial jar,

Like a bowstring snapped apart,
Like the daylight's broken heart.

Darkness leaps to have its way,
And the door swings to on day.

Creator! if Thy children might
Take such a clean leave of the light!
                    Robert P. Tristram Coffin

THE OWL

The sweet and ghostly laughter of the owl
Last night shook upward from the light bamboo.
The garden rose and trembled at the sound,
Suspended in enchantment and in dew.
What strange reversal of the blood and soul,
What dizzy floating upward from the earth,
When suddenly the darkness broke in two
Upon the honeyed edge of this soft mirth,
And in its wake a glint of mockery
Unbearable to hearts worn out with prayer.
For man, asleep, still labours over fears
The dreamless owl abandons to the air.
                    Hildegarde Flanner

THE DOWNY OWL

The downy owl, gray banshee of the night,
Weaving his lilt of sorrow to and fro

In the dim dawning, ere the crimson glow
Leads lusty day across the fields of light,
Awakes me with his melancholy rite,
His tremulous adagio, sweet and low,
As one who mourns a passion old as woe,
Or would too late a wounded love requite.
Hark how he whimpers in the brooding gloom,
Mocking lost joy — the still, forsaken room,
The unpressed pillow where no dear head lies!
Gray banshee owl, prophet of morning skies,
Proclaim the light, and let lost rapture be
One with the forest's gloom and mystery.
Edith Willis Linn

THE OWL

When cats run home and light is come,
   And dew is cold upon the ground,
And the far-off stream is dumb,
   And the whirring sail goes round,
   And the whirring sail goes round;
Alone and warming his five wits,
The white owl in the belfry sits.

When merry milkmaids click the latch,
   And rarely smells the new-mown hay,
And the cock hath sung beneath the thatch
   Twice or thrice his roundelay,
   Twice or thrice his roundelay;
Alone and warming his five wits,
The white owl in the belfry sits.

Alfred Tennyson

THE HORNÈD OWL

In the hollow tree, in the old grey tower,
   The spectral owl doth dwell;
Dull, hated, despised in the sunshine hour,
   But at dusk he's abroad and well:
Not a bird of the forest e'er mates with him,
   All mock him outright by day;
But at night when the woods grow still and dim,
   The boldest will shrink away.
     Oh, when the night falls, and roosts the fowl,
     Then, then is the reign of the hornèd owl!

And the owl hath a bride who is fond and bold,
   And loveth the wood's deep gloom;
And with eyes like the shine of the moonshine cold
   She awaiteth her ghostly groom!
Not a feather she moves, nor a carol she sings,
   As she waits in her tree so still;
But when her heart heareth his flapping wings,
   She hoots out her welcome shrill!
     Oh, when the moon shines and the dogs do howl,
     Then, then is the cry of the hornèd owl!

Mourn not for the owl nor his gloomy plight!
   The owl hath his share of good:
If a prisoner he be in the broad daylight,
   He is lord in the dark green wood!
Nor lonely the bird, nor his ghostly mate;
   They are each unto each a pride —
Thrice fonder, perhaps, since a strange dark fate
   Hath rent them from all beside!
     So when the night falls, and the dogs do howl,
     Sing ho! for the reign of the hornèd owl!

We know not alway who are kings by day,
But the king of the night is the bold brown owl.
Bryan Waller Procter

OWL SINISTER

Ah, can you never still,
Unhealable complainer of the wounded will?
   You groan-in-the-dark,
   You sobber of no shape,
And strong negation of the lark!
   You wrong-recounter of no words!
     Ape
   Of lovely birds,
And hunchback of the singing breed!
You void! You, irremediable Need,
   Make nothing of desire.
With long, cold crying famine you put out the fire,
   And esperances of the day rescind.
Eater of shadows! Ghoul and gullet of the wind!
Rose O'Neill

CLERICS

*"And they were all like clerics clad
In habit sober to the eye."*

THE BLACKBIRD [1]

When smoke stood up from Ludlow
  And mist blew off from Teme,
And blithe afield to ploughing
  Against the morning beam
  I strode beside my team,

The blackbird in the coppice
  Looked out to see me stride,
And hearkened as I whistled
  The trampling team beside,
  And fluted and replied:

"Lie down, lie down, young yeoman;
  What use to rise and rise?
Rise man a thousand mornings
  Yet down at last he lies,
  And then the man is wise."

I heard the tune he sang me,
  And spied his yellow bill;
I picked a stone and aimed it
  And threw it with a will:
  Then the bird was still.

Then my soul within me
  Took up the blackbird's strain,
And still beside the horses
  Along the dewy lane
  It sang the song again:

[1] The English blackbird belongs to the thrush family, and is a more accomplished singer than any of the American blackbirds.

"Lie down, lie down, young yeoman;
  The sun moves always west;
The road one treads to labor
  Will lead one home to rest,
  And that will be the best."

A. E. Housman

THE BLACKBIRD

The nightingale has a lyre of gold,
  The lark's is a clarion call,
And the blackbird plays but a boxwood flute,
  But I love him best of all.

For his song is all of the joy of life,
  And we in the mad, spring weather,
We two have listened till he sang
  Our hearts and lips together.

William Ernest Henley

THE BLACKBIRD

In the far corner
close by the swings,
every morning
a blackbird sings.

His bill's so yellow,
his coat's so black,
that he makes a fellow
whistle back.

Ann, my daughter,
thinks that he
sings for us two
especially.

Humbert Wolfe

TO AN IRISH BLACKBIRD

Wet your feet, wet your feet,
  That is what he seems to say,
Calling from the dewy thicket
  At the breaking of the day.

Wet your feet, wet your feet,
  Silver-toned he sounds the call
From his bramble in the thicket
  When the dew is on the fall.

Many times in lands far distant,
  In my dreams I hear him play
On his flute within the thicket,
  Ere the showers have passed away.

Years have passed since last I heard him,
  Since I said a sad adieu
To the early Irish morning
  With the rainbow-tinted dew.

And I still can hear him calling
  And the call comes clear and sweet,
And I still can see the mornings
  With the dew about my feet.

Wet your feet, wet your feet,
    Silver-toned he sounds the call
From his bramble in the thicket
    When the dew is on the fall.
James MacAlpine

BLACKBIRD

He comes on chosen evenings,
My blackbird bountiful, and sings
Over the gardens of the town
Just at the hour the sun goes down.
His flight across the chimneys thick,
By some divine arithmetic,
Comes to his customary stack,
And couches there his plumage black;
And there he lifts his yellow bill,
Kindled against the sunset, till
These suburbs are like Dymock woods
Where music has her solitudes,
And while he mocks the winter's wrong
Rapt on his pinnacle of song,
Figured above our garden plots
Those are celestial chimney-pots.
John Drinkwater

THE BLACKBIRD

*"I could not think so plain a bird
    Could sing so fine a song."*

One on another against the wall
Pile up the books, — I am done with them all!
I shall be wise, if I ever am wise,
Out of my own ears, and of my own eyes.

A MARSH BLACKBIRD

One day of the woods and their balmy light, —
One hour on the top of a breezy hill,
There in the sassafras all out of sight
The blackbird is splitting his slender bill
For the ease of his heart.

                Do you think if he said
I will sing like this bird with the mud-colored back
And the two little spots of gold over his eyes,
Or like to this shy little creature that flies
So low to the ground, with the amethyst rings
About her small throat, — all alive when she sings
With a glitter of shivering green, — for the rest,
Gray shading to gray, with the sheen of her breast
Half rose and half fawn, —

                Or like this one so proud,
That flutters so restless, and cries out so loud,
With still horny beak and a topknotted head,
And a lining of scarlet laid under his wings, —
Do you think, if he said, "I'm ashamed to be black!"
That he could have shaken the sassafras tree
As he does with the song he was born to? Not he!

Alice Cary

A MARSH BLACKBIRD

You of the crimson wing,
   Very spirit and breath
Of the ecstasy of spring,
What do I hear you sing
   At the darkling winter's death?

Just the old mad mirth
   That the ancient Aryans heard
In the primal days of earth!
After the long white dearth
   It is enough, O bird!

Harriet Sennett

A BLACKBIRD SUDDENLY

HEAVEN is in my hand, and I
Touch a heart-beat of the sky,
Hearing a blackbird's cry.

Strange, beautiful, unquiet thing,
Lone flute of God, how can you sing
Winter to spring?

You have out-distanced voice and word,
And given my spirit wings until it stirred
Like you — a bird!

Joseph Auslander

PURPLE GRACKLES

A CROSS between blackbird and crow
They say you are, and they should know.
Yet I insist your ancestors
Were never dusky troubadours
Of harshness only, but were found
Beating passage underground,
Crying sharply through the night
For young Persephone's delight,

For Queen Persephone's recalling
Now the purple wings come falling
Every May to one bent tree —
  Grackles for Persephone!

A cross between blackbird and crow
They say you are, and they should know.
I see you jaunty heretics
Whose fathers fanned the muddy Styx!
Frances M. Frost

PURPLE GRACKLES

The grackles have come.
The smoothness of the morning is puckered with their incessant chatter.
A sociable lot, these purple grackles,
Thousands of them strung across a long run of wind,
Thousands of them beating the air-ways with quick wing-jerks,
Spinning down the currents of the South.
Every year they come,
My garden is a place of solace and recreation evidently,
For they always pass a day with me.
With high good nature they tell me what I do not want to hear.
The grackles have come.

I am persuaded that the grackles are birds;
But when they are settled in the trees,
I am inclined to declare them fruits
And the trees turned hybrid blackberry vines.

Blackness shining and bulging under leaves,
Does not that mean blackberries, I ask you?
Nonsense! The grackles have come.

Nonchalant highwaymen, pickpockets, second-story burglars,
Stealing away my little hope of Summer.
There is no stealthy robbing in this.
Whoever heard such a gabble of thieves' talk!
It seems they delight in unmasking my poor pretense.
Yes, now I see that the hydrangea blooms are rusty;
That the hearts of the golden-glow are ripening to lustreless seeds;
That the garden is dahlia-coloured,
Flaming with its last over-hot hues;
That the sun is pale as a lemon too small to fill the picking-ring.
I did not see this yesterday,
But to-day the grackles have come.

They drop out of the trees
And strut in companies over the lawn,
Tired of flying no doubt;
A grand parade to limber legs and give wings a rest.
I should build a great fish-pond for them,
Since it is evident that a bird-bath, meant to accommodate two gold-finches at most,
Is slight hospitality for these hordes.
Scarcely one can get in,
They all peck and scrabble so,
Crowding, pushing, chasing one another up the bank with spread wings.
"Are we ducks, you owner of such inadequate comforts,

PURPLE GRACKLES

That you offer us lily-tanks where one must swim or drown,
Not stand and splash like a gentleman?"
I feel the reproach keenly, seeing them perch on the edges of the tanks, trying the depth with a chary foot,
And hardly able to get their wings under water in the bird-bath.
But there are resources I have not considered,
If I am bravely ruled out of count.
What is that thudding against the eaves just beyond my window?
What is that spray of water blowing past my face?
Two — three — grackles bathing in the gutter,
The gutter providentially choked with leaves.
I pray they think I put the leaves there on purpose;
I would be supposed thoughtful and welcoming
To all guests, even thieves.
But considering that they are going South and I am not,
I wish they would bathe more quietly,
It is unmannerly to flaunt one's good fortune.

They rate me of no consequence,
But they might reflect that it is my gutter.
I know their opinion of me,
Because one is drying himself on the window-sill
Not two feet from my hand.
His purple neck is sleek with water,
And the fellow preens his feathers for all the world as if I were a fountain statue.
If it were not for the window,
I am convinced he would light on my head.
Tyrian-feathered freebooter,

Appropriating my delightful gutter with so extravagant an ease,
You are as cool a pirate as ever scuttled a ship,
And are you not scuttling my Summer with every peck of your sharp bill?

But there is a cloud over the beech-tree.
A quenching cloud for lemon-livered suns.
The grackles are all swinging in the tree-tops.
And the wind is coming up, mind you.
That boom and reach is no Summer gale,
I know that wind,
It blows the Equinox over seeds and scatters them,
It rips petals from petals, and tears off half-turned leaves.
There is rain on the back of that wind.
Now I would keep the grackles,
I would plead with them not to leave me.
I grant their coming, but I would not have them go.
It is a milestone, this passing of grackles.
A day of them, and it is a year gone by.
There is magic in this and terror,
But I only stare stupidly out of the window.
The grackles have come.

Come! Yes, they surely came.
But they have gone.
A moment ago the oak was full of them,
They are not there now.
Not a speck of a black wing,
Not an eye-peep of a purple head.
The grackles have gone,
And I watch an Autumn storm

Stripping the garden,
Shouting black rain challenges
To an old, limp Summer
Laid down to die in the flower-beds.
Amy Lowell

THE CROW

My friend and neighbor through the year,
Self-appointed overseer

Of my crops of fruit and grain,
Of my woods and furrowed plain,

Claim thy tithings right and left,
I shall never call it theft.

Nature wisely made the law,
And I fail to find a flaw

In thy title to the earth,
And all it holds of any worth.

I like thy self-complacent air,
I like thy ways so free from care,

Thy landlord stroll about my fields,
Quickly noting what each yields;

Thy courtly mien and bearing bold,
As if thy claim were bought with gold;

Thy floating shape against the sky,
When days are calm and clouds are high;

Thy thrifty flight ere rise of sun,
Thy homing clans when day is done.

Hues protective are not thine,
So sleek thy coat each quill doth shine.

Diamond black to end of toe,
Thy counter-point the crystal snow.

Friendly bandit, Robin Hood,
Judge and jury of the wood,

Or Captain Kidd of sable quill,
Hiding treasures in the hill.

Nature made thee for each season,
Gave thee wit for ample reason,

Good crow wit that's always burnished
Like the coat her care has furnished.

May thy numbers ne'er diminish,
I'll befriend thee till life's finish.

May I never cease to meet thee,
May I never have to eat thee.

And mayst thou never have to fare so
That thou playest the part of scarecrow!
John Burroughs

CROW

A HUNDRED autumns he has wheeled
Above this solitary field.

Here he circled after corn
Before the oldest man was born.
When the oldest man is dead,
He will be unsurfeited.
See him crouch upon a limb
With his banquet under him.
Hear the echo of his caw
Give the skirting forest law.
Down he drops, and struts among
The rows of supper, tassel-hung.
Not a grain is left behind
That his polished beak can find.
He is full; he rises slow
To watch the evening come and go.
From the barren branch, his rest,
All is open to the west;
And the light along his wing
Is a sleek and oily thing.
Past an island floats the gaze
Of this ancientest of days.
Green and orange and purple dye
Is reflected in his eye.
There is an elm-tree in the wood
Where his dwelling-place has stood
All the hundreds of his years.
There he sails and disappears.
Mark Van Doren

SERFS

WINTER has planted the field black with crows.
In frustrate flocks they cark and scream and caw,
Plucking at furrow and frozen hill breast
For sustenance, without rest.

They caw their hunger upon the cold wind
That chaps the frosty skin of the brown earth;
They scream their hatred of hardship and strife
For mere food, mere life.

Black and bitter serfs, bound to the soil,
They hate mankind for what men take away
In overlord fashion — never knowing how little
Fills many a pot or kettle.

Bound to the soil, with a bleak enmity
Against us, for they are reapers of reaped lands,
They cry the old cry that God does less than well
To make an earth that can be made a hell.
Cale Young Rice

ROOKS

There, where the rusty iron lies,
    The rooks are cawing all the day.
Perhaps no man, until he dies,
    Will understand them, what they say.

The evening makes the sky like clay.
    The slow wind waits for night to rise.
The world is half content. But they

Still trouble all the trees with cries.
    They know, and cannot put away,
The yearning to the soul that flies
    From day to night, from night to day.
Charles Hamilton Sorley

THE BALLIOL ROOKS

The winter is dead, and the spring is a-dying,
    And summer is marching o'er mountain and plain,
And tossing and tumbling and calling and crying
    The Balliol rooks are above us again;
And watching them wheel on unwearied wings,
I question them softly of vanished things.

> *Caw, caw, says every rook,*
> *To the dreamer his dream, to the scholar his book.*
> *Caw, caw, but the things for me*
> *Are the windy sky and the windy tree!*

O rooks, have you leant from your heights and harkened
    From year to year to the whirl below?
While the suns have flamed and the days have darkened,
    Have you marked men ceaselessly come and go,
Loiter a little while here and pass
As the ripple on water, the shadow on grass?

The monk with his orisons heavenward rolling,
    The friar of black, and the friar of grey;
The schoolman stern, and the cavalier trolling
    In court and in cloister his roundelay,
The singer sweet and the preacher pale —
O rooks, can you tell me their wondrous tale?

And we that are heirs to their paths and places,
    To the alleys dim and the sunlit towers,
With our hearts on fire, and our eager faces,
    Still hasting along with the hasting hours;

O rooks, I pray you, come, tell me true:
Was it better the old? is it better the new?

And they that shall follow upon us hereafter,
   The men unknown of the unborn years;
Will they move you at all with their grief and laughter,
   Will you reck, O rooks, of their hopes and fears?
Or will you but circle scornfully,
And mock at them as you mock at me?

   Caw, caw, says every rook,
   To the dreamer his dream, to the scholar his book.
   Caw, caw, but the things for me
   Are the windy sky and the windy tree!
                                   Frederick S. Boas

THE ROOK SITS HIGH

The rook sits high, when the blast sweeps by,
   Right pleased with his wild see-saw;
And though hollow and bleak be the fierce wind's shriek,
   It is mocked by his loud caw-caw.
What careth he for the bloom-robed tree,
   Or the rose so sweet and fair?
He loves not the sheen of the spring-time green,
   Any more than the branches bare.
Oh! the merriest bird the woods e'er saw,
Is the sable rook with his loud caw-caw!

Winter may fling crystal chains on the wing
   Of the fieldfare, hardy and strong;
The snow-cloud may fall like a downy pall,
   Hushing each warbler's song;

The starved gull may come from his ocean home
    And the poor little robin lie dead;
The curlew bold may shrink from the cold,
    And the house-dove droop his head:
But the sable rook still chatters away,
Through the bitterest frost and the darkest day.

He builds not in bowers 'mid perfume and flowers,
    But as far from the earth as he can;
He weathers the storm, he seeks for the worm,
    And craves not the mercy of man.
Then a health to the bird whose music is heard
    When the ploughboy's whistle is still:
To the pinions that rise, when the hail-shower flies,
    And the moor-cock broods under the hill:
For the merriest fellow the woods e'er saw
Is the sable rook with his loud caw-caw.

Eliza Cook

ROOKS: NEW COLLEGE GARDENS

THROUGH rosy cloud and over thorny towers,
Their wings with darkling autumn distance filled,
From Isis' valley border, many-hilled,
The rooks are crowding home as evening lowers:
Not for men only, and their musing hours
By battled walls did gracious Wykeham build
These dewy spaces early sown and stilled,
These dearest inland melancholy bowers.

Blest birds! A book held open on the knee
Below, is all they guess of Adam's blight:
With surer art the while, and simpler rite,
They gather power in some monastic tree

Where breathe against their docile breasts by night
The scholar's star, the star of sanctity.

Louise Imogen Guiney

NESTS IN ELMS

The rooks are cawing up and down the trees!
Ripe as old music is the summer's measure
Of love, of all the busy-ness of leisure,
With dream on dream of never-thwarted ease!
O homely birds, whose cry is harbinger
Of nothing sad, who know not anything
Of sea-birds' loneliness, of Procne's strife,
Rock round me when I die! So sweet it were
To lie by open doors, with you on wing
Humming the deep security of life.

Michael Field

TROPICAL BIRDS

"Peacocks trail the glory of the world."

THE BIRD OF PARADISE

Fiery bitter blue it burns
Against the mountain's snow,
Pale eyries of the scaly rocks
Take color from its glow.
Where the tall trees break the air,
Its cry is clear.

Hunters falter in the climb,
Tremulous is that place
Where the burning feathers flutter,
And sink in space.
The bird has a strange note
Of terror in its throat.

From distant India it flew
One rainbow-colored spring
That tinged its youth with ecstasy, —
It strove to sing,
And flung itself to soar
Where the deep forests are.

Dumbly in cold sunlight
Spirit haunted sits the bird,
Beating upon unmeaning hours
To wrench one crystal word.
Gazing on the hollow skies
For immortality it cries.

Laura Benét

THE SILVER TREE

I wish that I could see to-night
  That tree in Cairo near the Nile,
On which at dusk the egrets light
  And sleep awhile.

At earliest dawn they fly away
  Into the desert, who knows where?
And the great dark-leaved tree all day
  Stands blossom-bare.

But when dusk folds the citadel
  Within Mokattan hills, it brings
To that expectant tree the thrill
  Of homing wings.

Down the long reaches of the Nile
  The silver birds come winging home
Past Boulac and Gezireh's isle,
  Past mosque and dome.

And suddenly the tree is drest
  In a white radiance of bloom,
As bird on bird drops down to rest
  With folded plume.

The gentle moon upon her way
  Looks down, and watches with delight
The silver tree, so bare by day,
  Blossom all night.

Francis Keppel

IBIS

Why were you hailed a sacred thing
   In the vague past without a date,
Bird of the seldom-lifted wing
   And form attenuate?

Though you are not hailed holy now
   You still keep something of that day
When Isis heard the suppliant's vow,
   And Thebes held regal sway.

Thoth and Osiris both are gone,
   And Memnon of the golden strain,
While in the clear Egyptian dawn
   You — only you remain.

Anonymous

FLAMINGOES

Over the wide reach of emerald rushes
   Where the waters of old Nilus pour,
Tinted as with rosy sunrise flushes
   Silent wing they toward the Libyan shore.

Types they are of mystery and wonder
   As all else within this hoary land, —
Pyramid and pylon rent asunder,
   And the tawny, ever-shifting sand.

Radiant, remote and sense-evading,
   They are like a dream at which we joyed,
Flashing on the vision and then fading
   In the golden-blue Egyptian void.

Harriet Sennett

WHITE PEACOCKS

Once at Isola Bella,
  With sunset in the sky,
We stood on the topmost terrace —
  You and I.

Around us Lago Maggiore,
  Incomparably fair,
Gave back the hues of heaven
  To the Italian air.

Then up the marble terrace,
  Below the cypress trees,
Came a flock of milk-white peacocks
  With fans spread to the breeze.

Rose-pink on each outspread feather,
  Rose-pink upon the crest —
Never were birds in plumage
  So ravishingly drest!

Wherever we walked, they followed,
  Stately at our feet;
No picture so enchanting
  Will any hour repeat.

And here in the murky city
  Those milk-white peacocks seem
To follow and follow me ever,
  Like ghosts of a haunting dream.

Jessie B. Rittenhouse

WHITE PEACOCK

(In Fontainebleau)

Ghost —
Bird of the Louis'
Powdered for a wig —
The blood of what delicate dynasties
Smirches so lightly
The intricate mist of your fan?
Ghost —
Walk silently
Upon the deserted lawns,
Lift each foot slowly to peer
Sidewise,
As an old Marquise
Spreading a skirt of silver lace,
For whom there is no longer
Surprise at anything
But only pride
And fear —
Wise bird, wise —
Between the marble urns you pause
(Finely veined and cracked with the moss
That spells their doom already).
When they are perished,
And even the terrace has fallen,
White peacocks will come from the groves
Silently
To step, elaborately poising, among their ruined
    particles.

You, whose dim ancestress
Was chained to the frail arched wrist
Of a king's exquisite harlot —

> Do you walk that way,
> Halting intricately,
> To show you once were chained?
>
> *Brenham McKay*

THE PARROT

The old professor of Zoölogy
Shook his long beard and spake these words to me:
"Compare the parrot with the dove. They are
In shape the same: in hue dissimilar.
The Indian bird, which may be sometimes seen
In red or black, is generally green.
His beak is very hard: it has been known
To crack thick nuts and penetrate a stone,
Alas, that when you teach him how to speak
You find his head is harder than his beak!
The passionless Malay can safely drub
The pates of parrots with an iron club:
The ingenious fowls, like boys they beat at school,
Soon learn to recognize a Despot's rule.

Now if you'd train a parrot, catch him young,
While soft the mouth and tractable the tongue.
Old birds are fools: they dodder in their speech,
More eager to forget than you to teach;
They swear one curse, then gaze at you askance,
And all oblivion thickens in their glance.

Thrice blest whose parrot of his own accord
Invents new phrases to delight his Lord,
Who spurns the dull quotidian task and tries
Selected words that prove him good and wise.

Ah, once it was my privilege to know
A bird like this...

> But that was long ago!"
> *James Elroy Flecker*

PRETTY POLLY

An agile noisy jungle flower he flies
Where monkeys pelt fierce peccaries with nuts;
And alligators lurk for chance supplies
'Neath river villages of tree-top huts.

When the Brazilian sun — a red-hot drum —
Rises, he screams a challenge with gold beak
To tell the jungle that the day is come;
Then preens each crimson feather with a tweak.

Fed with Andean milk, the Amazon
Glitters between the forests where he dines;
He gathers golden fruit or lunches on
The lustrous berries of vanilla vines.

He shouts at pythons looped like harmless boughs,
Or the poor sleepy sloths that scarcely move;
He ruffles plumes and utters lyric vows
To tell some pretty parrot flirt his love.

And he will guard, a brilliant sentinel,
The hollow nest where, in a warm round egg,
His son lies prisoner in a quiet cell,
Waiting his scarlet wing, his golden leg.

And when the sun, like some red armadillo,
Burrows into the West and birds must doze,

Cushioned all night upon an airy pillow
The parrot sleeps — except his gripping toes.

． ． ． ． ． ． ． ． ． ．

But someday it may be a Caliban
Will capture him and sell him to a cage
In our grey North, and make brass bars the span
Of one who had a jungle heritage.

Bird of bronze lyrics once, who blazed and flew,
He will become a thing of solemn folly
To please old maids or yokels at a zoo:
He'll ask for crackers and say, "Pretty Polly!"
                                    E. Merrill Root

DOVES AND WOODPECKERS

*"They go forgot in sky, but they will drift
Together downward and sink suddenly
To flutter at my feet like blossoms blown
From a high windy tree."*

"A crested woodpecker all trig and trim."

DOVES

Ah, if man's boast and man's advance be vain,
And yonder bells of Bow, loud-echoing home,
And the lone Tree, foreknow it, and the Dome,
That monstrous island of the middle main;
If each inheritor must sink again
Under his sires, as falleth where it clomb
Back on the gone wave the disheartened foam? —
I crossed Cheapside, and this was in my brain.

What folly lies in forecasts and in fears!
Like a wide laughter sweet and opportune,
Wet from the fount, three hundred doves of Paul's
Shook their warm wings, drizzling the golden noon,
And in their rain-cloud vanished up the walls.
"God keeps," I said, "our little flock of years."
Louise Imogen Guiney

THE WOOD-DOVE'S NOTE

Meadows with yellow cowslips all aglow,
   Glory of sunshine on the uplands bare,
And faint and far, with sweet elusive flow,
   The wood-dove's plaintive call,
                    "O where! where! where!"

Straight with old Omar in the almond grove
   From whitening boughs I breathe the odors rare
And hear the princess mourning for her love
   With sad unwearied plaint,
                    "O where! where! where!"

New madrigals in each soft pulsing throat —
New life upleaping to the brooding air —
Still the heart answers to that questing note,
  "*Soul of the vanished years,*
            O where! where! where!"
                    Emily Huntington Miller

WHITE DOVE OF THE WILD DARK EYES

White Dove of the wild dark eyes,
Faint silver flutes are calling
From the night where the star-mists rise
  And fireflies falling
  Tremble in starry wise.
  Is it you they are calling?

White Dove of the beating heart,
Shrill golden reeds are thrilling
In the wood where the shadows start,
  While moonbeams, filling
  With dreams the floweret's heart
  Its dreams are thrilling.

White Dove of the folded wings,
Soft purple night is crying
With the voice of fairy things
  For you, lest dying
  They miss your flashing wings,
  Your splendorous flying.
                    Joseph Mary Plunkett

THE MOURNING DOVE

Sweet is the hermit's evening bell,
And sweet the mellow canticle
Of the wood thrush; but more I love
The murmur of the mourning dove.

'Tis he awakes the vague unrest
That makes one wander east and west —
The fond, fond bird, tender and true,
He'll take the very heart from you.

O whirring wings! O trembling throat
That puts such heartbreak in a note!
All through the woodland shadows dim,
My heart is glad to follow him.

O soft and low! — but I'll no more
Over the ferny forest floor
At dawn or dusk to listen lest
He pluck the heart out of my breast.
W. W. Christman

THE COURTYARD PIGEONS

Dear birds, that flutter happily
   Against the grey stone wall
That hides the joyous sun from me,
   Do you not hear my call?
Each weary day when you go past
   To strut and perch up there,
Or when you soar away so fast,
   I watch you, and I care:

For, in your iridescent flight,
    My eyes have learned to see
How, in this strange and fearful night,
    One thing, at least, goes free.
And do you know what you have taught
    In low and cooing cries?
Though much is gone, they have not bought
    The part of me that flies!

Caroline Giltinan

PIGEONS

At morning the pale pigeons come in a band,
Shining and fleet, descending lightly where
I walk through red metallic tulips grown
High in the yellow air.

When they are here my garden is never my own.
I am a newcomer in a silent land.
And after I have gone the birds will run
About, the tulips stand.

The level breeze is silent in the sun.
The beautiful birds flock down; I cannot bear
Their folded ivory wings, I cannot ponder
Their hard incurious stare.

They peck possessive on the ground. I wander
Slow and persistent over grass and stone
Softly to scatter them until they lift
And I am left alone.

They go forgot in sky, but they will drift
Together downward and sink suddenly
To flutter at my feet like blossoms blown
From a high windy tree.

George Dillon

A VISIT WITH A WOODPECKER

I CAN recall an orchard gnarled and old
Where round plump pippins showed their cheeks of gold
Amid the leafage one ripe autumn day.
A crooked lane had led my steps that way,
And scaling the low barrier of a stile
I wandered down the deeply-fruited aisle.
There was no voice to cry me yea or nay
Till suddenly, as I strayed on, I heard
A most insistent tapping overhead
As though "Who comes? who comes?" some one had said.
I paused and listened. Was the sound a bird?
Yes, for I saw above me on a limb
A crested woodpecker all trig and trim
Who craned his neck and cocked a gleaming eye.
"Don't be afraid!" I called, "it's only I!"
He seemed quite satisfied with my reply.
"All right!" he tapped. We visited, and he
Showed me odd things I had not dreamed to see:
His store of grubs, his lodging for the night,
His treasure there — four eggs of snowy white;
And then we parted. —— Memory avers
That I learned much about sleek woodpeckers.

Charles Commerford

THE DOWNY WOODPECKER

Downy came and dwelt with me,
  Taught me hermit lore;
Drilled his cell in oaken tree
  Near my cabin door.

Architect of his own home
  In the forest dim,
Carving its inverted dome
  In a dozy limb.

Carved it deep and shaped it true
  With his little bill;
Took no thought about the view,
  Whether dale or hill.

Shook the chips upon the ground,
  Careless who might see,
Hark! his hatchet's muffled sound
  Hewing in the tree.

Round his door as compass-mark,
  True and smooth his wall;
Just a shadow on the bark
  Points you to his hall.

Downy leads a hermit life
  All the winter through;
Free his days from jar and strife,
  And his cares are few.

Waking up the frozen woods,
  Shaking down the snows;

THE DOWNY WOODPECKER

Many trees of many moods
    Echo to his blows.

Rat-tat-tat his chisel goes,
    Cutting out his prey;
Every boring insect knows
    When he comes its way.

Why does Downy live alone
    In his snug retreat?
Has he found that near the bone
    Is the sweetest meat?

Birdie craved another fate
    When the spring had come;
Advertised him for a mate
    On his dry-limb drum.

Drummed her up and drew her near,
    In the April morn,
Till she owned him for her dear
    In his state forlorn.

Now he shirks all family cares,
    This I must confess;
Quite absorbed in self affairs
    In the season's stress.

We are neighbors well agreed
    Of a common lot;
Peace and love our only creed
    In this charmèd spot.

John Burroughs

THE HEART OF YOUTH

Yellow-hammer's rat-tat-too on the orchard bough;
  That's the sound that used to break through my morning dreams;
Heigho! heart of youth! when I hear it now
  Back again my boyhood comes; very near it seems.

Through the prismy dews of morn I am out again;
  Rat-tat-too! that's the lure; straight my foot it leads;
Down the garden path I leap, — through the pasture lane;
  Heigho! heart of youth! Joy alone it heeds.

There he is (rat-tat-too!) yonder on the limb!
  Cap of red upon his head drumming in the day.
(Five white eggs are hidden deep in a hollow dim!)
  Heigho! heart of youth! Can't you hear him play?

Yellow-hammer, you and I in the long ago
  Cronies were; (rat-tat-too down the morning tossed!)
Here's a hail across the years, — how they fleetly flow! —
  Heigho! heart of youth! never wholly lost!

Anonymous

BIRDS OF PREY

"Hawks stir the blood like fiercely ringing bells."

GOLDEN FALCON

He sees the circle of the world
    Alive with wings that he
Was born to rend; his eyes are stars
    Of amber cruelty.

God lit the fire in his eyes
    And bound swords on his feet,
God fanned the furnace of his heart
    To everlasting heat.

His two eyes take in all the sky,
    East, West, North and South,
Opposite as poles they burn;
    And death is in his mouth.

Death because his Master knew
    That death is last and best,
Because He gives to those He loves
    The benison of rest.

Golden, cruel word of God
    Written on the sky!
Living things are lovely things,
    And lovely things must die.
                  Robert P. Tristram Coffin

THE HAWK

The hawk slipped out of the pine, and rose in the sunlit air:
    Steady and still he poised; his shadow slept on the grass:

And the bird's song sickened and sank: she cowered with furtive stare,
  Dumb, till the quivering dimness should flicker and shift and pass.

Suddenly down he dropped: she heard the hiss of his wing,
  Fled with a scream of terror: oh, would she had dared to rest!
For the hawk at eve was full, and there was no bird to sing,
  And over the heather drifted the down from a bleeding breast.

Arthur Christopher Benson

HAWK

I SEE you dart, swift pirate of the air,
  Swooping upon your unsuspecting prey,
  A dusky blot upon the face of day,
Eager to seize, unpitying to spare,
And fain to take your victim unaware
  As it pursues its unprotected way;
  A sudden waft of wings — a dire dismay —
And then the inevitable and dark despair.

Thus Death and Life, pursuer and pursued,
  While travailing man upon the earth draws breath;
Calm for a space and the contented mood,
  Then as the years pass, and time gathereth,
The stir of pinions and the certitude
  Of the sharp talons and the clutch of Death.

Clinton Scollard

THE HAWK

Thou dost not fly, thou art not perched,
    The air is all around:
What is it that can keep thee set,
    From falling to the ground?
The concentration of thy mind
    Supports thee in the air;
As thou dost watch the small young birds
    With such a deadly care.

My mind has such a hawk as thou,
    It is an evil mood;
It comes when there's no cause for grief,
    And on my joys doth brood.
Then do I see my life in parts;
    The earth receives my bones,
The common air absorbs my mind —
    It knows not flowers from stones.

William H. Davies

HAWK AFIELD

The quail are still.
Coveys are still.
The sparrows might be under ground.
Quail and young partridges have ceased to run;
Because of that violence,
Minute upon a peak of air,
Flashing, black-bladed,
Like an evil knife.
High up,
Unaided,
Flickering and isolated,

Burns,
Against the flexing turmoil after rain,
The black flame on the vast altar
Garnished for the sacrifice!
Dead grass, herbage, hedge, water,
A pond tweaked by the breeze and afterglow,
Reflect — Him!
He burns up the soul of peaceful countryside.
His is the attention of a universe.

He falls.
Heaven plunges with him.
The fixed meadows all collapse.

It is over for the other —
Not for the hawk,
Once more a flicker and bereft of victim
In this still land where all is enemy,
Fierce, obdurate and only half defeated,
In motion no more than a twinge,
He stands alone to hold the sky.

Evelyn Scott

THE BUZZARDS

When evening came and the warm glow grew deeper,
And every tree that bordered the green meadows
And in the yellow cornfields every reaper
And every corn-shock stood above their shadows
Flung eastward from their feet in longer measure,
Serenely far there swam in the sunny height
A buzzard and his mate who took their pleasure
Swinging and poising idly in golden light.

On great pied motionless moth-wings borne along,
So effortless and strong,
Cutting each other's paths together they glided,
Then wheeled asunder till they soared divided
Two valleys' width (as though it were delight
To part like this, being sure they could unite
So swiftly in their empty, free dominion),
Curved headlong downward, towered up the sunny steep,
Then, with a sudden lift of the one great pinion,
Swung proudly to a curve, and from its height
Took half a mile of sunlight in one long sweep.

And we, so small on the swift immense hillside,
Stood tranced, until our souls arose uplifted
On those far-sweeping, wide,
Strong curves of flight — swayed up and hugely drifted,
Were washed, made strong and beautiful in the tide
Of sun-bathed air. But far beneath, beholden
Through shining depths of air, the fields were golden
And rosy burned the heather where cornfields ended.

And still those buzzards whirled, while light withdrew
Out of the vales and to surging slopes ascended,
Till the loftiest flaming summit died to blue.

Martin Armstrong

THE FISH-HAWK

On the large highway of the awful air that flows
  Unbounded between sea and heaven, while twilight screened
The majestic distances, he moved and had repose;

THE FISH-HAWK

On the huge wind of the Immensity he leaned
His steady body in long lapse of flight — and rose

Gradual, through broad gyres of ever-climbing rest,
   Up the clear stair of the eternal sky, and stood
Throned on the summit! Slowly, with his widening breast,
   Widened around him the enormous Solitude,
From the gray rim of ocean to the glowing west.

Headlands and capes forlorn of the far coast, the land
   Rolling her barrens toward the south, he, from his throne
Upon the gigantic wind, beheld: he hung — he fanned
   The abyss for mighty joy, to feel beneath him strown
Pale pastures of the sea, with heaven on either hand —

The world with all her winds and waters, earth and air,
   Fields, folds, and moving clouds. The awful and adored
Arches and endless aisles of vacancy, the fair
   Void of sheer heights and hollows hailed him as her lord
And lover in the highest, to whom all heaven lay bare!

Till from that tower of ecstasy, that baffled height,
   Stooping, he sank; and slowly on the world's wide way
Walked, with great wing on wing, the merciless, proud Might,
   Hunting the huddled and lone reaches for his prey
Down the dim shore — and faded in the crumbling light.

Slowly the dusk covered the land. Like a great hymn
  The sound of moving winds and waters was; the sea
Whispered a benediction, and the west grew dim
  Where evening lifted her clear candles quietly....
Heaven, crowded with stars, trembled from rim to rim.

John Hall Wheelock

THE BLACK VULTURE

ALOOF upon the day's immeasured dome,
  He holds unshared the silence of the sky.
  Far down his bleak, relentless eyes descry
The eagle's empire and the falcon's home —
Far down, the galleons of sunset roam;
  His hazards on the sea of morning lie;
  Serene, he hears the broken tempest sigh
Where cold sierras gleam like scattered foam.

And least of all he holds the human swarm —
  Unwitting now that envious men prepare
    To make their dream and its fulfillment one,
When, poised above the caldrons of the storm,
  Their hearts, contemptuous of death, shall dare
    His roads between the thunder and the sun.

George Sterling

TURKEY-BUZZARDS

SILENTLY, every hour, a pair would rise
And float, without an effort, clear of the trees —
Float in a perfect curve, then tilt and drop;
Or tilt again and spiral toward the sun.

They might have been a dream the timber dreamed....
But could have been a conscious thought, that cut
The warm blue world in segments. For the sky,
Unmeasured, was too much that afternoon.
It lay too heavy on us.... Happy trees,
If they could so divide it, wing and wing!
Mark Van Doren

THE EAGLE

HE clasps the crag with crooked hands;
Close to the sun in lonely lands,
Ringed with the azure world, he stands.

The wrinkled sea beneath him crawls;
He watches from his mountain walls,
And like a thunderbolt he falls.
Alfred Tennyson

OSPREY AND EAGLE

ON a gaunt and shattered tree
By the black cliffs of obsidian
I saw the nest of the osprey.

Nothing remained of the tree
For this lonely eyrie
Save the undaunted bole
That cycles of winds had assaulted
And, clinging still to the bole,
Tenacious, the topmost branches.
Here, to scan all the heavens,
Nested the osprey.

On a rock by the rim of the canyon,
A rock standing stark and isolate,
I saw the nest of the eagle.

Nothing remained of the rock
Save what the jade-green river
Deep on the floor of the canyon
Had left in the ages' eroding.
This, with the ancient upheavals,
Had cut it sheer from its fellows.
Here, to scan all the heavens,
Nested the eagle.

My cringing soul
Was suddenly
Shamed into hardihood.
Jessie B. Rittenhouse

EAGLE

THE grim eagle —
Poets love him not,
Else had they oftener sung
His soaring flights.

Who are his lovers?

Mystics, artists, symbolists.
He is the bird of Manitou, the Great Spirit,
Climbing aloft to the celestial throne;
The bird of the Evangelist St. John,
Winged messenger of winged words divine.

He is the bird of bas-relief —
Of ancient tapestries,
Of goldsmith's craft,
Of the mintman's art:

He is the bird of empires and tyrannies,
Of Roman legions:
Two-headed eagle, sinister, of imperial pride
Now bowed in dust.

James B. Thomas

BIRDS OF THE SNOWY SOLSTICE

*"Yet all my hopes, like winter birds,
Sing on amid the snow."*

THE SNOW LIES LIGHT

The snow lies light upon the pine,
The winds are still, the day is fine;
My guests come trooping in to dine.
There are so many to be fed
I have a generous table spread
With corn and nuts and fat and seed
To suit each vagrant's taste and need.

From far and near the jays convene,
And redpolls leave the evergreen.
The finch that wears a splendid crown
Is also of the company.
Goldfinches with their gold turned brown,
Juncoes with peeping petticoats,
Tree sparrows lisping whispered notes,
With downy, nuthatch, chickadee,
I welcome to my almonry.

Now that the winter smooths and stills
My valley in the Helderhills
Not one that shares of my alms-deed
Will play a pipe or blow a reed.
All are so still I sometimes long
To hear the dear fox sparrow's song,
To see the purple finches wed
And whitethroat in tree sparrow's stead.
I'll ask the chickadee, he'll know
The time that rills shall fill and flow,
And hylas peep and soft winds blow.

Dear little wildwood bird! mayhap
There's wisdom under your black cap;

And will next week bring thaw and rain
And hints of April tints again —
Or do you deeper snow foresee?
"Knee deep! Knee deep!" said chickadee.
W. W. Christman

THE TREE OF STARLINGS

All the starlings in our town
Have settled in the hillside elm.
Since the last leaves were blown down
Only sunlight wraps each bough
In a gossamer of blue air,
And the leafy stars at night
Keep the tree from feeling bare:
But as thick as leaves just now
Came the birds to overwhelm
Any doubts the elm-tree had
With their whistles of delight.
What it is that makes them glad
I should tell you if I knew.
All this April rollicking
In the last month of the year
Has no logic I can see.
They must know it isn't Spring.
It's not as if they didn't know!
They expect to winter here;
They stay to emphasize the snow.
I suppose it can't be true
They are thronging there to make
Merry for the old elm's sake?
It isn't a kind of Christmas tree?
Grace Hazard Conkling

WINTER BIRDS

There was no covert for the birds
   And yet I heard them sing
As joyously as if the trees
   Were canopied with spring.

And though the way is still obscure
   That you and I must go,
Yet all my hopes, like winter birds,
   Sing on amid the snow.

Elinor MacArthur

CHICKADEES

Blackcap, madcap!
Never tired of play
What's the news to-day?
  "Faint-heart, faint-heart!
Winter's coming up this way;
And the winter comes to stay!"

Blackcap, madcap!
Whither will you go,
Now the storm winds blow?
  "Faint-heart, faint-heart!
In the pine-boughs, thick and low,
There is shelter from the snow!"

Blackcap, madcap!
In the snow and sleet,
What have you to eat?
  "Faint-heart, faint-heart.
Seeds and berries are a treat,
When the frost has made them sweet!"

Blackcap, madcap!
Other birds have flown
To a sunnier zone!
"Faint-heart, faint-heart!
When they're gone, we blackcaps own
Our white playground all alone!"

Edith M. Thomas

CHICKADEE

There's a hush on the frosty furrow where the frozen loam lifts black,
And a film on the brown hare's burrow unmarred by a seeking track,
And over the leafless uplands comes echoing clear to me
A voice from the edge of winter:
"Chickadee dee dee! Chickadee!"

The fox has slunk from the bracken with the flag of his tail dropped low,
And the whining hound-winds slacken at the first soft swirl of snow,
But still from the wind-blown whiteness comes cheerily back to me
A gay little voice from the pine-top:
"Chickadee dee dee! Chickadee!"

Oh, little gray Puck undaunted when the fields lie white and still,
May ever my pane be haunted by your voice at my window-sill,
The cheeriest note of winter comes rollicking oft to me
Like the voice of a song-struck sunbeam:
"Chickadee dee dee! Chickadee!"

Martha Haskell Clark

THE TITMOUSE

You shall not be overbold
When you deal with arctic cold,
As late I found my lukewarm blood
Chilled wading in the snow-choked wood.
How should I fight? my foeman fine
Has million arms to one of mine:
East, west, for aid I looked in vain,
East, west, north, south, are his domain.
Miles off, three dangerous miles, is home;
Must borrow his winds who there would come.

Softly, — but this way fate was pointing,
'Twas coming fast to such anointing,
When piped a tiny voice hard by,
Gay and polite, a cheerful cry,
Chic-chicadeedee! saucy note
Out of sound heart and merry throat,
As if it said, "Good day, good sir!
Fine afternoon, old passenger!
Happy to meet you in these places,
Where January brings few faces."

This poet, though he live apart,
Moved by his hospitable heart,
Sped, when I passed his sylvan fort,
To do the honors of his court,
As fits a feathered lord of land;
Flew near, with soft wing grazed my hand,
Hopped on the bough, then, darting low,
Prints his small impress on the snow,
Shows feats of his gymnastic play,
Head downward, clinging to the spray.

Here was this atom in full breath,
Hurling defiance at vast death;
This scrap of valor just for play
Fronts the north-wind in waistcoat gray,
As if to shame my weak behaviour;
I greeted loud my little saviour,
"You pet! what dost here? and what for?
In these woods, thy small Labrador,
At this pinch, wee San Salvador!
What fire burns in that little chest
So frolic, stout, and self-possest?

Henceforth I wear no stripe but thine;
Ashes and jet all hues outshine.
Why are not diamonds black and gray,
To ape thy dare-devil array?
And I affirm the spacious north
Exists to draw thy virtue forth.
I think no virtue goes with size;
The reason of all cowardice
Is, that men are overgrown,
And, to be valiant, must come down
To the titmouse dimension."

'Tis good-will makes intelligence,
And I began to catch the sense
Of my bird's song; "Live out of doors
In the great woods, on prairie floors.
I dine in the sun; when he sinks in the sea,
I too have a hole in a hollow tree;
And I like less when Summer beats
With stifling beams on these retreats,
Than noontide twilights which snow makes
With tempest of the blinding flakes.

THE TITMOUSE

For well the soul, if stout within,
Can arm impregnably the skin;
And polar frost my frame defied,
Made of the air that blows outside."

With glad remembrance of my debt,
I homeward turn; farewell, my pet!
When here again thy pilgrim comes,
He shall bring store of seeds and crumbs.
Doubt not, so long as earth has bread,
Thou first and foremost shalt be fed;
The Providence that is most large
Takes hearts like thine in special charge,
Helps who for their own need are strong,
And the sky dotes on cheerful song.
Henceforth I prize thy wiry chant
O'er all that mass and minster vaunt;
For men mis-hear thy call in spring,
As 'twould accost some frivolous wing,
Crying out of the hazel copse, *Phe-be!*
And, in winter, *Chic-a-dee-dee!*
I think old Cæsar must have heard
In northern Gaul my dauntless bird,
And, echoed in some frosty wold,
Borrowed thy battle-numbers bold.
And I will write our annals new,
And thank thee for a better clue,
I, who dreamed not when I came here
To find the antidote of fear,
Now hear thee say in Roman key,
Pæan! Veni, vidi, vici.

Ralph Waldo Emerson

INDEXES

INDEX OF FIRST LINES

A ball of fire shoots through the tamarack	114
A close gray sky	62
A cross between blackbird and crow	212
A day and then a week passed by	114
A golden day	160
A hundred autumns he has wheeled	218
A late lark twitters from the quiet skies	65
A lonely lake, a lonely shore	187
A meadow lark sang at the drooping of dusk	97
A Robin Redbreast in a cage	22
A strange thing, that a lark and robin sky	182
A thousand miles from land are we	166
A voice peals in this end of night	73
A wingèd rocket curving through	118
Across the narrow beach we flit	156
Across the noisy street	72
Ah, can you never still	204
Ah, if man's boast and man's advance be vain	237
Ah! say you so, bold sailor	178
All day long in the spindrift swinging	167
All the starlings in our town	260
All through the sultry hours of June	73
Along the sea-edge, like a gnome	158
Aloof upon the day's immeasured dome	253
An agile noisy jungle flower he flies	233
And after April, when May follows	71
And so, with feet God meant should cling	18
As it fell upon a day	78
At morning the pale pigeons come in a band	240
At play in April skies that spread	45
Beautiful must be the mountains whence ye come	85

INDEX OF FIRST LINES

Because you have no fear to mingle	43
Before you thought of spring	39
Bird of the fierce delight	161
Bird of the wilderness	55
Birds, companions more unknown	21
Birds that float upon a wave	164
Blackcap, madcap!	261
Blow softly, thrush, upon the hush	66
Can freckled August, — drowsing warm and blonde	105
Crescent-winged, sky-clean	189
Dancer of air	119
Day after day you who are as free as air	94
Dear birds, that flutter happily	239
Delay your flight, delay your swift pursuit	193
Devoutly worshiping the oak	100
Down from the sky on a sudden he drops	100
Downy came and dwelt with me	242
Ethereal minstrel! pilgrim of the sky	56
Faith, peace and joy to-day brings; all has failed	190
Fiery bitter blue it burns	227
For, singing till his heaven fills	64
From Casco Bay	76
Ghost	231
God bade the birds break not the silent spell	70
Good speed, for I this day	53
Gray geese over the rock-ribbed hill, solemnly	187
Hail to thee, blithe spirit!	56
Happy is he who lies awake	14
Hark! ah, the nightingale	83
Hark! hark! the lark at heaven's gate sings	53
Hark, 'tis the bluebird's venturous strain	38

INDEX OF FIRST LINES

Hawks stir the blood like fiercely ringing bells	192
He clasps the crag with crooked hands	254
He comes on chosen evenings	210
He sees the circle of the world	247
Hear! hear! hear!	125
Heaven is in my hand, and I	212
Here's a health to the birds one and all!	3
High at the window in her cage	19
His voice runs before me; I follow, it flies	32
How falls it, oriole, thou hast come to fly	111
How oft against the sunset sky or moon	182
I can recall an orchard gnarled and old	241
I have just seen three ducks rise up from the rushes	182
I have wished a bird would fly away	5
I hear a rainbird singing	34
I hear a savage tale of you	41
I hear the low wind wash the softening snow	184
I hear you, little bird	17
I heard a bird at break of day	6
I heard a wood-thrush in the dusk	68
I heard the wild geese flying	186
I hold to my heart when the geese are flying	186
I leant upon a coppice gate	74
I lift the latch	47
I saw with open eyes	22
I see you dart, swift pirate of the air	248
I thought to shoulder Time but those sad birds	27
I was on the ocean once	155
I watched the day come up the road	129
I will fare up White Creek Water	117
I wish that I could see to-night	228
If this be all, for which I've listened long	63
In came the moon and covered me with wonder	71
In Mercer Street the light slants down	63
In the far corner	208
In the hollow tree, in the old grey tower	203

INDEX OF FIRST LINES

In the middle of August when the southwest wind	145
Is this the lark	61
It is a wee, sad-colored thing	98
It pulses through the twilight	35
It was the Rainbow gave thee birth	191
It would take an angel's eye	117
June's bridesman, poet o' the year	101
Last night it was the whip-poor-will	198
Little brown surf-bather of the mountains!	189
Lone white gull with sickle wings	163
Look! the valleys are thick with grain	95
Lord of the odored alleys green! who on the silence flings	126
Meadows with yellow cowslips all aglow	237
Merrily swinging on brier and weed	101
My brave	68
My friend and neighbor through the year	217
My heart aches, and a drowsy numbness pains	80
Nightingale I never heard	138
No human lips caress	128
Not knowing he rose from earth, not having seen him rise	60
Now that the giant sunflowers rise	99
Now that the twilight slants the curled edges of wheat	97
O bird that somewhere yonder sings	12
O blithe new-comer! I have heard	31
O cuckoo troubling yonder hill	33
O lonely trumpeter, coasting down the sky	181
O lonesome sea-gull, floating far	163
O melancholy bird, a winter's day	173
O nightingale that on yon bloomy spray	79
O nightingale! thou surely art	84
O spark, you winged from secret woodland forges	113

INDEX OF FIRST LINES

"O spheral, spheral!" he seems to say	77
Oh, for a day in the white wind's cheek!	180
Oh, how they murdered poor Bob White to-day!	96
Oh, thou northland bobolink	104
Oh, you and I, wild thrush — we share	69
On a gaunt and shattered tree	254
On the crimson edge of the eve	86
On the large highway of the awful air that flows	251
Once at Isola Bella	230
One day, while still the dawn denied the call	173
One on another against the wall	210
Oriole — athlete of the air	111
Out of the cradle endlessly rocking	130
Out of what ancient summer of soft airs	197
Over the wide reach of emerald rushes	229
Pack, clouds, away, and welcome day	3
Prime indignity of solitude	158
Redbirds, redbirds	113
Sauntering hither on listless wings	154
Sea-gull swooping	162
Sea-mosses hide the massive architrave	28
Silently, every hour, a pair would rise	253
Softly at dawn a whisper stole	38
Summer is i-comen in	31
Superb and sole upon a plumèd spray	127
Sure maybe ye've heard the storm-thrush	36
Swallow, my sister, O sister swallow	48
Sweet is the hermit's evening bell	239
Tameless in his stately pride, along the lake of islands	187
Tell me, you	15
The downy owl, gray banshee of the night	201
The fierce musical cries of a couple of sparrow-hawks hunting on the headland	26

INDEX OF FIRST LINES

The geese drive northward	42
The grackles have come	213
The grim eagle	255
The hawk slipped out of the pine, and rose in the sunlit air	247
The herons on Bo Island	175
The lark knows no such rapture	153
The magpies in Picardy	107
The moonbeams over Arno's vale in silvery flood were pouring	67
The night-hawk goes up to the light	200
The nightingale has a lyre of gold	208
The nightingales at Fairford sing	85
The old Hercynian Forest sent	176
The old professor of Zoölogy	232
The quail are still	249
The robin is the one	35
The rooks are cawing up and down the trees	224
The rook sits high, when the blast sweeps by	222
The singing of birds is as certain as the long	6
The singing white-throat poured my gladness out	93
The snow lies light upon the pine	259
The sweet and ghostly laughter of the owl	201
The trees are in their autumn beauty	193
The wet sands were grey-blue that afternoon	162
The whip-poor-will, through the crystal starlight	199
The wild geese come over no more	185
The winter is dead, and the spring is a-dying	221
The wonder was on me in Curraghmacall	19
There is a singer everyone has heard	93
There was no covert for the birds	261
There's a hush on the frosty furrow where the frozen loam lifts black	262
There where the rusty iron lies	220
This is the way of a bird	14
Thou dost not fly, thou art not perched	249
Thou little bird, thou dweller by the sea	155

INDEX OF FIRST LINES 275

Thou who hast slept all night upon the storm	167
Through rosy cloud and over thorny towers	223
Through Tanglewood the thrushes trip	68
Time cannot age thy sinews, nor the gale	168
To give me its bright plumes they shot a jay	23
Under the eaves, out of the wet	98
Up with me! up with me into the clouds	54
Upon this leafy bush	93
Villon among the birds is he	41
Wet your feet, wet your feet	209
What do they here, these denizens of the deep	165
What I saw was just one eye	11
When cats run home and light is come	202
When cities prod me with demands	7
When early summer called us back	199
When evening came and the warm glow grew deeper	250
When ice is thawed and snow is gone	39
When June was cool and clover long	44
When languorous noons entreat the summer sky	121
When lilies by the river fill with sun	70
When smoke stood up from Ludlow	207
When the mild gold stars flower out	120
When the spring is fresh from the hand of God	37
When through the heaviness and clamouring throng	116
Where water-grass grows overgreen	174
White Dove of the wild dark eyes	238
Whither, midst falling dew	183
Who can be that somber fellow	139
Who sings upon the pinnacle of night?	197
Why were you hailed a sacred thing	229
Winged mimic of the woods! thou motley fool!	125
Winter has planted the field black with crows	219
With wings held close and slim neck bent	192
Within mankind's duration, so they say	23

INDEX OF FIRST LINES

Yellow-hammer's rat-tat-too on the orchard bough	244
Yes, Nightingale, through all the summer-time	87
You of the crimson wing	211
You shall not be overbold	263
You, who would with wanton art	140
Your carol is a dewy, fragrant bloom that grows	18

INDEX OF TITLES

A Bird Sings at Night. *Hildegarde Flanner*	197
A Blackbird Suddenly. *Auslander*	212
A Meadow Lark Sang. *Commerford*	97
Albatross. *Stoddard*	168
Articulate Thrush. *Sarett*	69
Ballade of the Thrush. *Dobson*	72
Balliol Rooks, The. *Boas*	221
Berceuse for Birds. *Auslander*	97
Bird at Dawn, The. *Monro*	11
Bird at Dawn, To a. *Le Gallienne*	12
Bird Music. *Rorty*	6
Bird of Paradise, The. *Laura Benét*	227
Bird on a Downtown Wire, To a. *Greer*	18
Bird Sings in the Night, A. *Hildegarde Flanner*	197
Bird Song. *Noyes*	15
Birds. *Jeffers*	26
Birds. *Moira O'Neill*	36
Birds, The. *Gorman*	27
Birds, The. *Squire*	23
Birds of Whitby, The. *T. S. Jones, Jr.*	28
Black Vulture, The. *Sterling*	253
Blackbird. *Drinkwater*	210
Blackbird. The. *Alice Cary*	210
Blackbird, The. *Henley*	208
Blackbird, The. *Housman*	207
Blackbird, The. *Wolfe*	208
Blackbird Suddenly, A. *Auslander*	212
Blow Softly, Thrush. *J. R. Taylor*	66
Blue Heron, The. *M. Thompson*	174
Blue Jay. *Leonora Speyer*	41
Blue Jay, The. *Louise Driscoll*	41
Blue Tit, To a. *Friedlaender*	94

INDEX OF TITLES

Bluebird, The. *Aldrich* 38
Bluebird, The. *Emily Dickinson* 39
Bluebird, The. *M. Thompson* 39
Bob White. *Dora Read Goodale* 95
Bobolink, The. *J. R. Lowell* 101
Buzzards, The. *Armstrong* 250

Caged Bird, A. *Sarah Orne Jewett* 19
Canticle. *Griffith* 100
Cardinal Bird, The. *Gallagher* 114
Catbird. *Crombie* 139
Catbird, My. *Venable* 138
Catbird, To the. *Anonymous* 140
Chickadee. *Martha Haskell Clark* 262
Chickadees. *Edith M. Thomas* 261
Courtyard Pigeons, The. *Caroline Giltinan* . . 239
Crow. *Van Doren* 218
Crow, The. *Burroughs* 217
Cuckoo. *Katherine Tynan Hinkson* 32
Cuckoo, The. *Le Gallienne* 33
Cuckoo, To the. *Wordsworth* 31
Cuckoo Song. *Anonymous* 31

Damascus Nightingale, A. *Crombie* 86
Darkling Thrush, The. *Hardy* 74
Dawn in the Everglades. *Warlow* 173
Death of a Favorite Canary, On the. *Matthew Arnold* . 21
Doves. *Louise Imogen Guiney* 237
Downy Owl, The. *Edith Willis Linn* 201
Downy Woodpecker, The. *Burroughs* . . . 242

Eagle. *J. B. Thomas* 255
Eagle, The. *Tennyson* 254
Etching at Dusk. *Prokosch* 182

Fairford Nightingales. *Drinkwater* 85
Fish-Hawk, The. *Wheelock* 251
Flamingoes. *Harriet Sennett* 229

INDEX OF TITLES

Flaw, A. *Michael Field*	23
Flight of the Geese, The. *Roberts*	184
Flute of Krishna, The. *J. B. Thomas*	128
Fox Sparrow, The. *Christman*	42
Golden Falcon. *Coffin*	247
Goldfinch, The. *Shepard*	100
Goldfinches. *Elisabeth Scollard*	99
Gray Geese Flying. *Prokosch*	187
Grosbeak in the Garden, To a. *I. Swift*	116
Gulls over Great Salt Lake. *Sutphen*	165
Happy is He. *Leonora Speyer*	14
Hawk. *C. Scollard*	248
Hawk, The. *Benson*	247
Hawk, The. *W. H. Davies*	249
Hawk Afield. *Evelyn Scott*	249
Health to the Birds, A. *MacManus*	3
Hearing a Bird Sing at Night, On. *Morton*	197
Heart of Youth, The. *Anonymous*	244
Herald Crane, The. *Garland*	178
Hermit Thrush in the Catskills, A. *Griffith*	77
Heron, The. *Hovell-Thurlow*	173
Herons on Bo Island, The. *Elizabeth Shane*	175
Hornèd Owl, The. *Procter*	203
Humming Bird. *Coffin*	117
Humming Bird, A. *Fawcett*	120
Humming Bird, The. *Ednah Proctor Clarke*	119
Humming Bird, The. *I. Swift*	121
Humming Bird, The. *M. Thompson*	118
Ibis. *Anonymous*	229
Indigo Bird. *Crombie*	117
Irish Blackbird, To an. *MacAlpine*	209
Is this the Lark. *Auslander*	61
Itylus. *Swinburne*	48
Joy of the Morning. *Markham*	17

INDEX OF TITLES

Kingfisher, The. *W. H. Davies*	191
Lapland Longspur, To the. *Burroughs*	104
Lark, The. *Lizette Woodworth Reese*	62
Lark, To the. *Herrick*	53
Lark Ascending, The. *Meredith*	64
Lark's Song. *O'Sullivan*	63
Last Bob White, The. *W. Montgomery*	96
Late Lark, A. *Henley*	65
Lesser Children, The. *R. Torrence*	145
Linnet, The. *De la Mare*	93
Little Beach-Bird, The. *Dana*	155
Lone Swan. *Rose Mills Powers*	193
Loon, The. *Sarett*	187
Loon, The. *Street*	187
Magpies in Picardy. *T. P. C. Wilson*	107
Man-of-War-Bird, To the. *Whitman*	167
Marsh Blackbird, A. *Harriet Sennett*	211
Meadow Lark Sang, A. *Commerford*	97
Minor Bird, A. *Frost*	5
Mocking Bird, The. *Bacheller*	126
Mocking Bird, The. *Hovey*	125
Mocking Bird, The. *Lanier*	127
Mocking Bird, To a. *Grover*	129
Mocking Bird, To the. *Wilde*	125
Morning Bird. *Untermeyer*	14
Mourning Dove, The. *Christman*	239
My Catbird. *Venable*	138
My Thrush. *M. Collins*	73
Nests in Elms. *Michael Field*	224
Night-Hawk. *Coffin*	200
Nightingale, The. *Barnfield*	78
Nightingale, To the. *Milton*	79
Nightingale Unheard, The. *Josephine Preston Peabody*	87
Nightingales. *Bridges*	85

INDEX OF TITLES

O Nightingale! thou surely art. *Wordsworth* . . . 84
Ode to a Nightingale. *Keats* 80
On First Having Heard the Skylark. *Edna St. Vincent Millay* 60
On Hearing a Bird Sing at Night. *Morton* . . . 197
On the Death of a Favourite Canary. *Matthew Arnold* 21
Onset, The. *Jessie B. Rittenhouse* 162
Oriole, To an. *Fawcett* 111
Osprey and Eagle. *Jessie B. Rittenhouse* . . . 254
Out of the Cradle Endlessly Rocking. *Whitman* . . 130
Oven-bird, The. *Frost* 93
Overtones. *Percy* 6
Owl, The. *Hildegarde Flanner* 201
Owl, The. *Tennyson* 202
Owl Sinister. *Rose O'Neill* 204

Pack, Clouds, Away. *Heywood* 3
Parrot, The. *Flecker* 232
Petrel, To a. *Rice* 167
Philomela. *M. Arnold* 83
Phœbe. *Anonymous* 98
Phœbe Bird, To a. *Bynner* 98
Pigeons. *Dillon* 240
Poet to Bird. *Cheyney* 18
Pretty Polly. *Root* 233
Purple Grackles. *Frances M. Frost* 212
Purple Grackles. *Amy Lowell* 213

Rainbird, The. *Carman* 34
Rain-Crow, The. *Cawein* 105
Redbirds. *Sara Teasdale* 113
Return to Birds. *Untermeyer* 7
Robert of Lincoln. *Bryant* 101
Robin, The. *Emily Dickinson* 35
Robin Song. *Elisabeth Scollard* 35
Rook Sits High, The. *Eliza Cook* 222
Rooks. *Sorley* 220

INDEX OF TITLES

Rooks: New College Gardens. *Louise Imogen Guiney* . 223

Sanctuary. *Elinor MacArthur* . 155
Sandpiper, The. *Bynner* . 158
Sandpiper, The. *Swift* . 158
Sandpiper, The. *Celia Thaxter* . 156
Scarlet Tanager, The. *Benton* . 114
Scarlet Tanager, To a. *Dresbach* . 113
Sea-Bird, To a. *Harte* . 154
Sea-Birds. *Elizabeth Akers Allen* . 163
Sea-Birds. *Elinor MacArthur* . 164
Sea-Gull. *Mary Carolyn Davies* . 162
Sea-Gull, To a. *Symons* . 161
Seamew, To a. *Swinburne* . 153
Sea-Stretch, *Rena Sheffield* . 160
Serfs. *Rice* . 219
Silver Tree, The. *Keppel* . 228
Skylark, The. *Hogg* . 55
Skylark, To a. *Shelley* . 56
Skylark, To a. *Wordsworth* . 54, 56
Snow Lies Light, The. *Christman.* . 259
Solitary Sea-Gull, To a. *Rice* . 163
Song from Cymbeline. *Shakespeare* . 53
Song of the Hermit Thrush, The. *J. B. Thomas* . 76
Song-Sparrow, The. *MacKaye* . 44
Southern Whip-poor-will, A. *C. Scollard* . 198
Sparrow, To a. *Ledwidge* . 43
Spring Song. *Griffith* . 38
Spring's Torch-Bearer. *M. Thompson* . 111
Stormy Petrel, The. *Procter* . 166
Stupidity Street. *Hodgson* . 22
Swallow, The. *Burroughs* . 45
Swan, The. *Elizabeth Coatsworth* . 192
Swans. *Leonora Speyer* . 192
Swifts in the Chimney. *Rose Mills Powers* . 47

The Rook Sits High. *Eliza Cook* . 222

INDEX OF TITLES

The Snow Lies Light. *Christman*	259
The Wild Geese Come Over No More. *Rice*	185
There are still Kingfishers. *A. Y. Campbell*	190
Three Things to Remember. *Blake*	22
Thrush, My. *M. Collins*	73
Thrush, The. *Laura Benét*	70
Thrush before Dawn, A. *Alice Meynell*	73
Thrush in the Moonlight, A. *Bynner*	71
Thrushes. *K. W. Baker*	68
Titmouse, The. *Emerson*	263
To a Bird at Dawn. *Le Gallienne*	12
To a Bird on a Downtown Wire. *Greer*	18
To a Blue Tit. *Friedlaender*	94
To a Grosbeak in the Garden. *I. Swift*	116
To a Mocking Bird. *Grover*	129
To a Petrel. *Rice*	167
To a Phœbe Bird. *Bynner*	98
To a Scarlet Tanager. *Dresbach*	113
To a Sea-Bird. *Harte*	154
To a Sea-Gull. *Symons*	161
To a Seamew. *Swinburne*	153
To a Skylark. *Shelley*	56
To a Skylark. *Wordsworth*	54, 56
To a Solitary Sea-Gull. *Rice*	163
To a Sparrow. *Ledwidge*	43
To a Waterfowl. *Bryant*	183
To a Wild Goose over Decoys. *Sarett*	181
To an Irish Blackbird. *MacAlpine*	209
To an Oriole. *Fawcett*	111
To an Upland Plover. *MacKaye*	189
To the Catbird. *Anonymous*	140
To the Cuckoo. *Wordsworth*	31
To the Lapland Longspur. *Burroughs*	104
To the Lark. *Herrick*	53
To the Man-of-War-Bird. *Whitman*	167
To the Mocking Bird. *Wilde*	125
To the Nightingale. *Milton*	79

INDEX OF TITLES

Tree of Starlings, The. *Grace Hazard Conkling* . . 260
Tryst, The. *W. Montgomery* 37
Turkey-Buzzards. *Van Doren* 253
Two Nests, The. *Carlin* 19

Upland Plover, To an. *MacKaye* 189

Veery, The. *Van Dyke* 67
Village Stork, The. *B. Taylor* 176
Visit with a Woodpecker, A. *Commerford* . . 241

Water Ouzel, The. *Harriet Monroe* 189
Waterfowl, To a. *Bryant* 183
Whip-poor-will. *Cummings* 199
Whip-poor-will, The. *Anonymous* 199
White Dove of the Wild Dark Eyes. *Plunkett* . 238
White Peacock. *McKay* 231
White Peacocks. *Jessie B. Rittenhouse* . . . 230
White-throat, The. *Anonymous* 93
Wild Duck, The. *McLeod* 182
Wild Geese. *Eleanor Chipp* 186
Wild Geese. *Grace Noll Crowell* 186
Wild Geese. *Peterson* 182
Wild Geese Come Over No More, The. *Rice* . . 185
Wild Goose over Decoys, To a. *Sarett* . . . 181
Wild Swans at Coole, The. *Yeats* 193
Winter Birds. *Elinor MacArthur* 261
Wise Thrush, The. *Browning* 71
With the Mallard Drake. *Anonymous* . . . 180
Wood-Dove's Note, The. *Emily Huntington Miller* 237
Wood Song. *Sara Teasdale* 68
Wood-Thrush. *C. Scollard* 68
Wood-Thrush, The. *Cheney* 70
Word with a Skylark, A. *Sarah M. B. Piatt* . . 63

INDEX OF AUTHORS

ALDRICH, THOMAS BAILEY
  The Bluebird 38
ALLEN, ELIZABETH AKERS
  Sea-Birds 163
ANONYMOUS
  Cuckoo Song 31
  The White-throat 93
  Phœbe 98
  To the Catbird 140
  With the Mallard Drake 180
  The Whip-poor-will 199
  The Heart of Youth, ... 244
  Ibis 229
ARMSTRONG, MARTIN
  The Buzzards 250
ARNOLD, MATTHEW
  On the Death of a Favourite Canary 21
  Philomela 83
AUSLANDER, JOSEPH
  Is this the Lark 61
  Berceuse for Birds 97
  A Blackbird Suddenly 212

BACHELLER, IRVING
  The Mocking Bird 126
BAKER, KARLE WILSON
  Thrushes 68
BARNFIELD, RICHARD
  The Nightingale 78
BENÉT, LAURA
  The Thrush 70
  The Bird of Paradise 227

INDEX OF AUTHORS

BENSON, ARTHUR CHRISTOPHER
  The Hawk 247
BENTON, JOEL
  The Scarlet Tanager 114
BLAKE, WILLIAM
  Three Things to Remember 22
BOAS, FREDERICK S.
  The Balliol Rooks 221
BRIDGES, ROBERT
  Nightingales 85
BROWNING, ROBERT
  The Wise Thrush 71
BRYANT, WILLIAM CULLEN
  To a Waterfowl 183
  Robert of Lincoln 101
BURROUGHS, JOHN
  The Swallow 45
  To the Lapland Longspur 104
  The Downy Woodpecker 242
  The Crow 217
BYNNER, WITTER
  A Thrush in the Moonlight 71
  To a Phœbe Bird 98
  The Sandpiper 158

CAMPBELL, A. Y.
  There are still Kingfishers 190
CARLIN, FRANCIS
  The Two Nests 19
CARMAN, BLISS
  The Rainbird 34
CARY, ALICE
  The Blackbird 210
CAWEIN, MADISON
  The Rain-Crow 105
CHENEY, JOHN VANCE
  The Wood-Thrush 70

INDEX OF AUTHORS

CHEYNEY, RALPH
   Poet to Bird 18
CHIPP, ELEANOR
   Wild Geese 186
CHRISTMAN, W. W.
   The Fox Sparrow 42
   The Mourning Dove 239
   The Snow Lies Light 259
CLARKE, EDNAH PROCTOR
   The Humming Bird 119
CLARKE, MARTHA HASKELL
   Chickadee 262
COATSWORTH, ELIZABETH
   The Swan 192
COFFIN, ROBERT P. TRISTRAM
   Golden Falcon 247
   Humming Bird 117
   Night-Hawk 200
COLLINS, MORTIMER
   My Thrush 73
COMMERFORD, CHARLES
   A Meadow Lark Sang 97
   A Visit with a Woodpecker 241
CONKLING, GRACE HAZARD
   The Tree of Starlings 260
COOK, ELIZA
   The Rook sits High 222
CROMBIE, STEPHEN
   A Damascus Nightingale 86
   Indigo Bird 117
   Catbird 139
CROWELL, GRACE NOLL
   Wild Geese 186
CUMMINGS, PHILIP
   Whip-poor-will 199

DANA, RICHARD HENRY
   The Little Beach-Bird 155

INDEX OF AUTHORS

DAVIES, MARY CAROLYN
   Sea-gull 162
DAVIES, WILLIAM H.
   The Kingfisher 191
   The Hawk 249
DE LA MARE, WALTER
   The Linnet 93
DICKINSON, EMILY
   The Robin 35
   The Bluebird 39
DILLON, GEORGE
   Pigeons 240
DOBSON, AUSTIN
   Ballade of the Thrush 72
DRESBACH, GLENN WARD
   To a Scarlet Tanager 113
DRINKWATER, JOHN
   Fairford Nightingales 85
   Blackbird 210
DRISCOLL, LOUISE
   The Blue Jay 41

EMERSON, RALPH WALDO
   The Titmouse 263

FAWCETT, EDGAR
   To an Oriole 111
   A Humming Bird 120
FIELD, MICHAEL
   A Flaw 23
   Nests in Elms 224
FLANNER, HILDEGARDE
   A Bird Sings at Night 197
   The Owl 201
FLECKER, JAMES ELROY
   The Parrot 232
FRIEDLAENDER, V. H.
   To a Blue Tit 94

INDEX OF AUTHORS

FROST, FRANCES M.
   Purple Grackles 212
FROST, ROBERT
   A Minor Bird 5
   The Oven-bird 93

GALLAGHER, WILLIAM DAVIS
   The Cardinal Bird 114
GARLAND, HAMLIN
   The Herald Crane 178
GILTINAN, CAROLINE
   The Courtyard Pigeons 239
GOODALE, DORA READ
   Bob White 95
GORMAN, HERBERT
   The Birds 27
GREER, HILTON R.
   To a Bird on a Downtown Wire 18
GRIFFITH, WILLIAM
   Spring Song 38
   A Hermit Thrush in the Catskills 77
   Canticle 100
GROVER, EDWIN OSGOOD
   To a Mocking Bird 129
GUINEY, LOUISE IMOGEN
   Rooks: New College Gardens 223
   Doves 237

HARDY, THOMAS
   The Darkling Thrush 74
HARTE, FRANCIS BRET
   To a Sea-Bird 154
HENLEY, WILLIAM ERNEST
   A Late Lark 65
   The Blackbird 208
HERRICK, ROBERT
   To the Lark 53

INDEX OF AUTHORS

HEYWOOD, THOMAS
 Pack, Clouds, Away 3
HINKSON, KATHERINE TYNAN
 Cuckoo 32
HODGSON, RALPH
 Stupidity Street 22
HOGG, JAMES
 The Skylark 55
HOUSMAN, A. E.
 The Blackbird 207
HOVELL-THURLOW, EDWARD
 The Heron 173
HOVEY, RICHARD
 The Mocking Bird 125

JEFFERS, ROBINSON
 Birds 26
JEWETT, SARAH ORNE
 A Caged Bird 19
JONES, THOMAS S., JR.
 The Birds of Whitby 28

KEATS, JOHN
 Ode to a Nightingale 80
KEPPEL, FRANCIS
 The Silver Tree 228

LANIER, SIDNEY
 The Mocking Bird 127
LEDWIDGE, FRANCIS
 To a Sparrow 43
LE GALLIENNE, RICHARD
 To a Bird at Dawn 12
 The Cuckoo 33
LINN, EDITH WILLIS
 The Downy Owl 201
LOWELL, AMY
 Purple Grackles 213

INDEX OF AUTHORS

LOWELL, JAMES RUSSELL
   The Bobolink 101

MACALPINE, JAMES
   To an Irish Blackbird 209

MACARTHUR, ELINOR
   Sanctuary 155
   Sea-Birds 164
   Winter Birds 261

MACKAYE, PERCY
   The Song-Sparrow 44
   To an Upland Plover 189

MACMANUS, SEUMAS
   A Health to the Birds 3

MARE, WALTER DE LA
   The Linnet 93

MARKHAM, EDWIN
   Joy of the Morning 17

MCKAY, DANIEL BRENHAM
   White Peacock 231

MCLEOD, LEROY
   The Wild Duck 182

MEREDITH, GEORGE
   The Lark Ascending 64

MEYNELL, ALICE
   A Thrush Before Dawn 73

MILLAY, EDNA ST. VINCENT
   On First Having Heard the Skylark 60

MILLER, EMILY HUNTINGTON
   The Wood-Dove's Note 237

MILTON, JOHN
   To the Nightingale 79

MONROE, HARRIET
   The Water Ouzel 189

MONRO, HAROLD
   The Bird at Dawn 11

MONTGOMERY, WHITNEY
   The Last Bob White 96

INDEX OF AUTHORS

    The Tryst 37
MORTON, DAVID
    On Hearing a Bird Sing at Night 197

NOYES, ALFRED
    Bird Song 15

O'NEILL, MOIRA
    Birds 36
O'NEILL, ROSE
    Owl Sinister 204
O'SULLIVAN, SEUMAS
    Lark's Song 63

PEABODY, JOSEPHINE PRESTON
    The Nightingale Unheard 87
PERCY, WILLIAM ALEXANDER
    Overtones 6
PETERSON, FREDERICK
    Wild Geese 182
PIATT, SARAH M. B.
    A Word with a Skylark 63
PLUNKETT, JOSEPH MARY
    White Dove of the Wild Dark Eyes 238
POWERS, ROSE MILLS
    Swifts in the Chimney 47
    Lone Swan 193
PROCTER, BRYAN WALLER
    The Stormy Petrel 166
    The Hornèd Owl 203
PROKOSCH, FREDERICK
    Etching at Dusk 182
    Gray Geese Flying 187

REESE, LIZETTE WOODWORTH
    The Lark 62
RICE, CALE YOUNG
    To a Solitary Sea-Gull 163

INDEX OF AUTHORS

To a Petrel	167
The Wild Geese Come Over No More	185
Serfs	219

RITTENHOUSE, JESSIE B.
The Onset	162
Osprey and Eagle	254
White Peacocks	230

ROBERTS, CHARLES G. D.
The Flight of the Geese	184

ROOT, E. MERRILL
Pretty Polly	233

RORTY, JAMES
Bird Music	6

SARETT, LEW
Articulate Thrush	69
The Loon	187
To a Wild Goose over Decoys	181

SCOLLARD, CLINTON
Wood-Thrush	68
A Southern Whip-poor-will	198
Hawk	248

SCOLLARD, ELISABETH
Robin Song	35
Goldfinches	99

SCOTT, EVELYN
Hawk Afield	249

SENNETT, HARRIET
A Marsh Blackbird	211
Flamingoes	229

SHAKESPEARE, WILLIAM
Song from Cymbeline	53

SHANE, ELIZABETH
The Herons on Bo Island	175

SHEFFIELD, RENA CARY
Sea-Stretch	160

SHELLEY, PERCY BYSSHE
To a Skylark	56

INDEX OF AUTHORS

SHEPARD, ODELL
  The Goldfinch 100
SORLEY, CHARLES HAMILTON
  Rooks 220
SPEYER, LEONORA
  Blue Jay 41
  Happy is He 14
  Swans 192
SQUIRE, J. C.
  The Birds 23
STERLING, GEORGE
  The Black Vulture 253
STODDARD, CHARLES WARREN
  Albatross 168
STREET, ALFRED BILLINGS
  The Loon 187
SUTPHEN, ROSS
  Gulls over Great Salt Lake 165
SWINBURNE, ALGERNON CHARLES
  Itylus 48
  To a Seamew 153
SWIFT, IVAN
  To a Grosbeak in the Garden 116
  The Humming Bird 121
  The Sandpiper 158
SYMONS, ARTHUR
  To a Sea-Gull 161

TAYLOR, BAYARD
  The Village Stork 176
TAYLOR, JOSEPH RUSSELL
  Blow Softly, Thrush 66
TEASDALE, SARA
  Wood Song 68
  Redbirds 113
TENNYSON, ALFRED
  The Owl 202

INDEX OF AUTHORS

   The Eagle 254
THAXTER, CELIA
   The Sandpiper 156
THOMAS, EDITH M.
   Chickadees 261
THOMAS, JAMES B.
   The Song of the Hermit Thrush 76
   The Flute of Krishna 128
   Eagle 255
THOMPSON, MAURICE
   The Bluebird 39
   Spring's Torch-Bearer 111
   The Humming Bird 118
   The Blue Heron 174
TORRENCE, RIDGELY
   The Lesser Children 145

UNTERMEYER, LOUIS
   Morning Bird 14
   Return to Birds 7

VAN DOREN, MARK
   Crow 218
   Turkey-Buzzards 253
VAN DYKE, HENRY
   The Veery 67
VENABLE, WILLIAM HENRY
   My Catbird 138

WARLOW, HALLE W.
   Dawn in the Everglades 173
WHEELOCK, JOHN HALL
   The Fish-Hawk 251
WHITMAN, WALT
   To the Man-of-War-Bird 167
   Out of the Cradle Endlessly Rocking 130
WILDE, RICHARD HENRY
   To the Mocking Bird 125

INDEX OF AUTHORS

WILSON, T. P. CAMERON
   Magpies in Picardy 107
WOLFE, HUMBERT
   The Blackbird 208
WORDSWORTH, WILLIAM
   To the Cuckoo 31
   To a Skylark 54
   To a Skylark 56
   O Nightingale! thou surely art 84

YEATS, WILLIAM BUTLER
   The Wild Swans at Coole 193

INDEX OF BIRDS

Albatross, 168, 169

Bird of paradise, 227
Blackbird (American), 210-12
Blackbird, European, 4, 25, 67, 207-10
Blackbird, red-winged, 8, 211, 212
Bluebird, 6, 10, 38-40
Bobolink, 9, 101-04
Bob-white, 95, 96
Buzzard, European, 250, 251
Buzzard, turkey, 253, 254

Canary, 19-21
Cardinal, 8, 114, 115. See also Redbird
Catbird, 8, 138-41
Chat, yellow-breasted, 9
Chebec, 9
Chickadee, 98, 259-65
Cormorant, 26
Crane, 178, 179
Crow, American, 9, 217-20
Cuckoo (American). See Rain-crow
Cuckoo, European, 31-34
Cushadoo, 36. See also Pigeon, wood

Dipper, American. See Water-ouzel
Dove, domestic, 237-40

Dove, mourning, 239
Dove, stock, 84
Dove, wood, 237, 238. See also Cushadoo and Pigeon, wood
Ducks, wild, 182. See also Mallard

Eagles, 254-56
Egret (Egyptian), 228
Egret, snowy. See Heron, snowy

Falcon, 247
Flamingo (Egyptian), 229
Flicker, or yellow-hammer, 244

Goldfinch, American, 8, 99, 100
Goose, Canada, 181, 184-86
Goose (European), 182, 183
Goose, gray, 187
Grackle, 10
Grackle, purple, 212-16
Grosbeak, rose-breasted, 116
Grouse, ruffed, or partridge, 9
Gulls, 25-27, 161-65. See also Seamew

Hawk, American sparrow, 26, 27

INDEX OF BIRDS

Hawk, fish, or osprey, 251–54
Hawks, 247–50
Heron, great blue, 174
Heron, snowy, 174
Herons, 173, 175
Hummingbird, ruby-throated, 8, 9, 117–21

Ibis, sacred, 229
Indigo-bird, 117

Jay, blue, 9, 41, 42
Jay, European, 23

Kildee, 37, 38
Kingbird, 9
Kingfisher, European, 190, 191

Lark. *See* Skylark
Laverock, 67. *See also* Skylark
Leverock, 4. *See also* Skylark
Linnet, 4, 93, 94
Longspur, Lapland, 104, 105
Loon, 187, 188

Magpie, European, 107, 108
Mallard, 180, 181
Man-o'-war-bird, 167, 168
Martin, European house, 25
Martin, purple, 9
Mavis, 4. *See also* Thrush, European song.
Meadowlark, 8, 97
Mockingbird, 125–38

Nighthawk, 9, 200, 201
Nightingale, 67, 78–90

Oriole, Baltimore, 8, 111, 112
Osprey, *or* fish hawk, 251–54
Oven-bird, 8, 93
Owl, barn *or* white (European), 202
Owl, horned (European), 203
Owls, 201, 202, 204

Parrots, 232–34
Partridge. *See* Grouse, ruffed
Peacock, 230, 231
Pelican, 160
Petrel, 167
Petrel, stormy, 166, 167
Pewee, wood, 9
Phœbe, 9, 98, 99
Pigeon, domestic, 237–40
Pigeon, wood, 25. *See also* Cushadoo *and* Dove, wood
Plover, killdeer, 37, 38
Plover, upland, 189, 190

Rain-crow, 105–07
Redbird, 113. *See also* Cardinal
Redbreast. *See* Robin, European
Redstart, American, 8
Robin, American, 8, 35
Robin, European, 22, 36
Rook, 25, 220–24

Sandpiper, 156–59
Sea-Gull. *See* Gull

INDEX OF BIRDS

Seamew, 153. *See also* Gull
Skylark, *or* laverock (leverock), 4, 19, 22, 25, 53–67
Sparrow, chipping, 8
Sparrow, field, 10
Sparrow, fox, 42, 43
Sparrow, house, 8, 25, 43, 44
Sparrow, song, 44, 45
Sparrow, white-throated, 6
Starling, 260
Stork, 176–78
Swallow, barn, 45–47
Swallow, European, 48–50
Swallows (American), 8
Swans, 192–94
Swift, chimney, 9, 47, 48

Tanager, 9
Tanager, scarlet, 113, 114
Thrasher, brown, 8
Throstle, 28. *See also* Thrush, European song
Thrush, European song, 25, 36, 71–75
Thrush, hermit, 10, 76–78
Thrush, missel, *or* storm, 36
Thrush, tawny. *See* Veery

Thrush, wood, 68–70
Thrushes (American), 68, 70, 71
Tit, 25
Tit, blue, 94, 95
Titmouse. *See* Chickadee

Veery, 10, 66, 67
Vireo, 7, 10
Vulture, black, 253
Vulture, turkey, *or* turkey buzzard, 253, 254

Water-hen, 24
Water-ouzel, 189
Whip-poor-will, 9, 198–200
White-throat, 93. *See also* Sparrow, white-throated.
Woodpecker, 241
Woodpecker, downy, 242, 243
Wren, European, 5, 19, 22, 25
Wrens (American), 9

Yellow-hammer, *or* flicker, 244
Yellow-throat, 9